D0028166

WANTING ENLIGHTENMENT
IS A BIG MISTAKE

Also by Zen Master Seung Sahn

The Compass of Zen

Only Don't Know: Selected Teaching Letters of
Zen Master Zeung Sahn

The Whole World Is a Single Flower:
365 Kong-Ans for Everyday Life

Dropping Ashes on the Buddha:
The Teaching of Zen Master Seung Sahn

Bone of Space: Poems of Zen Master Seung Sahn

Wanting Enlightenment Is a Big Mistake

TEACHINGS OF ZEN MASTER SEUNG SAHN

COMPILED AND EDITED BY
Hyon Gak

Foreword by Jon Kabat-Zinn

SHAMBHALA
BOSTON & LONDON
2006

Shambhala Publications, Inc.
Horticultural Hall
300 Massachusetts Avenue
Boston, Massachusetts 02115
www.shambhala.com

9 8 7 6 5 4 3 2 1

First Edition
Printed in the United States of America

⊗ This edition is printed on acid-free paper that meets
the American National Standards Institute z39.48 Standard.
Distributed in the United States by Random House, Inc.,
and in Canada by Random House of Canada Ltd

Designed by Graciela Galup

Library of Congress Cataloging-in-Publication Data
Sungsan [Seung Sahn] Tae Sonsa.
Wanting enlightenment is a big mistake: the teachings of zen master
Seung Sahn.
p.   cm.
Original title unknown.
ISBN-13: 978-1-59030-340-5 (alk. paper)
ISBN-10: 1-59030-340-7
1. Zen Buddhism. 2. Spiritual life—Buddhism. 3. Sungsan Tae Sonsa.
I. Title.
BQ9266.S92 2006
294.3′420427—dc22
2006000545

CONTENTS

CONTENTS

FOREWORD

Zen Master Seung Sahn first came into my life in 1971. I was teaching at Brandeis at the time, and one of my students told me about a Korean Zen master she had been studying with in Providence, Rhode Island, at a Zen center he had established there. She said he was quite a character, with an unusual teaching style. He was not to be missed, for the show of it, if for no other reason, and she recommended that I check him out, knowing of my strong interest in Zen. So I went. And it all turned out to be true.

Soen Sa Nim, as he was known to his students at the time, was indeed a character. Very informal, he often sat around in what can only be described as "monk-leisurewear," when he wasn't wearing his formal robes. He hardly knew English, but that didn't stop him from teaching in English anyway. His shear determination to communicate the Dharma and his Zen perspective to Americans overcame any liability stemming from his lack of fluency. The fact that English grammar eluded him almost completely made his teaching even more powerful and unique. You really had to drop underneath his words to grasp his true intention and meaning. But he said things so powerfully and so uniquely that, after a while, they took on a life of their own, in a language all their own that gradually or suddenly found its way into our hearts and into our bones. His teaching often made an end run around our thinking minds and intellects, which were perpetually flummoxed by his efforts to circumvent them or cancel them out completely. It was like swallowing one hologram and another, like great poetry, and feeling them blossom inwardly, revealing a rich dimensionality we were somehow missing in our highly regimented and quotidian lives.

This book is the first collection of Soen Sa Nim's Dharma talks and other material to be published since his death, and it is likely the last to be gathered together at his behest by his first generation of Western students. You will notice that certain phrases and themes repeat over and over again. That is because Soen Sa Nim actually said them over and over again in his Dharma talks. One such phrase is "You must attain 'no attainment.'" Another is, "Open your mouth and you're wrong." He was always talking about "not making things." "Don't make anything" he would say. Not I-me-my; good, bad; me, you; difficult, easy; Buddha, enlightenment; the examples would go on and on. It was his way of saying that the truth is "before thinking." "Just keep clear mind, go straight ahead, try, try, try for ten thousand years," or from moment to moment for that matter—they were the same to him— because he wasn't "making" time either: "Only just like this!" "This *ouch* (after hitting a student—symbolically) is your original mind."

His exchanges with those who came to hear him and had the temerity to ask him questions and engage in his Zen dialogues were sometimes illuminating, sometimes confusing, but always compelling . . . leaving the whole room feeling that these koans were lingering, tweaking the ways we would relate to our interior experience on the cushion, and in our lives. For example:

Q: Is there such a thing as a clean mind?

A: If you have a mind, then you must clean your mind. If you have no mind, cleaning is not necessary. So I ask you, do you have a mind?

And on it would go. As long as we were trying to understand or respond out of thought, we were in deep trouble. It just wasn't possible. But the "primary point," as he liked to call it, kept manifesting out of all these paradoxical exchanges and teachings. "Who are you?" "Don't know." "You must keep this 'don't know mind.'" Only when he said it, it came out sounding more like "Donnnnno."

His irreverence was fantastic. It was so outrageous, it took on the qualities of a reverence all its own. For example (from page 27 in this book):

> This is a very interesting try-mind story. It means, from moment to moment only *do* it. Only keep a try-mind, only one mind: only *do-it* mind. When chanting, or sitting, or bowing, even special practicing cannot help you if you are attached to your thinking. Taoist chanting, Confucian chanting, Christian chanting, Buddhist chanting don't matter. Chanting "Coca Cola, Coca Cola, Coca Cola . . ." can be just as good if you keep a clear mind. But if you don't keep a clear mind, and are only following your thinking as you mouth the words, even the Buddha cannot help you.

And then he lets us have it both barrels:

The most important thing is, only *do* it. When you only do something, 100 percent, then there is no subject, no object. There is no inside or outside. Inside and outside already become one. That means you and the universe are never separate. There is no thinking.

Soen Sa Nim was also a great storyteller. We never knew if his stories were true or not, but it really didn't matter. They were teaching stories, and they made their points by calling into question and disarming our tacit assumptions and belief systems, the very lenses we were holding up to perceive reality. He was using stories to show us how big our minds really are.

One night, with Soen Sa Nim sitting next to me, I gave the Wednesday evening public talk at the Cambridge Zen Center. When it was over, he answered the questions. It was his way of training his students to become teachers. It was a pretty interesting and challenging training regimen.

The very first question came from a young man halfway back in the audience, on the right side of the room, who, in the way he asked the question (I forget entirely what the import of it was), demonstrated a degree of psychological disturbance and confusion that caused a ripple of concern and curiosity to pass through the audience. As usually happens in such situations, many necks craned, as discreetly as possible of course, to get a look at who was speaking.

Soen Sa Nim gazed at this young man for a long time, peering over the rims of his glasses. Utter silence in the room. He massaged the top of his shaven head as he continued gazing at him. Then, with his hand still massaging his head, still peering over his glasses, with his body tilted slightly forward toward the speaker from his position sitting on the floor, Soen Sa Nim said, cutting to the chase as usual: "You craaazy!"

Sitting next to him, I gasped, as did the rest of the room. In an instant, the tension rose by several orders of magnitude. I wanted to lean over and whisper in his ear: "Listen, Soen Sa Nim, when somebody is really crazy, it's not such a good idea to say it in public like that. Go easy on the poor guy, for God's sake." I was mortified.

All of that transpired in my mind and probably the minds of everybody else in the room in one momentary flash. The reverberations of what he had just said were hanging in the air. But he wasn't finished.

After a silence that seemed forever, Soen Sa Nim continued: ". . . but . . . [another long pause] . . . you not crazy ennuffff."

Everybody breathed a sigh of relief, and a feeling of lightness spread through the room.

This interchange didn't follow a predictable script for meeting suffering with compassion, but I felt in that moment that everyone had participated in and witnessed an enormous embrace of compassion and loving-kindness, Soen Sa Nim–style.

There was a side of Soen Sa Nim that almost no one saw or knew until this book. It is revealed in his wild yet measured effort to speak truth to power in secretly writing to the Korean President, Chun Du-Hwan, who seized control of the country in a coup and ran a military dictatorship that killed hundreds and perhaps thousands of Koreans. In the last chapter in this volume, in Soen Sa Nim's "Letter to a Dictator," we are witness to a remarkable private attempt to communicate heart to heart with this ruthless leader, who, as Soen Sa Nim well knew, was nevertheless still a human being. Soen Sa Nim was offering Chun the nondual Dharma, stressing the necessity for understanding one's own mind and true self as the only path for shouldering the leadership of a nation in an ethical, responsible, and compassionate way. Straight talk from beginning to end. Pure Soen Sa Nim. Given the personal risks to himself, Soen Sa Nim clearly had a lot of courage, and obviously cared deeply about social and humanitarian issues, enough to put his own life on the line. I found it very moving to picture the meeting of these two, six years after Chun's fall and seclusion in internal exile, as Soen Sa Nim handed him a copy of the letter he had sent him years before, and sat there as Chun read this prescription for strong medicine that he never filled or swallowed.

Now that Soen Sa Nim is gone, we have only the stories, and, thankfully, books such as this one, to help bring him alive to those who never had a chance to encounter him in the flesh. In these pages, if you linger in them long enough and let them soak into you, you will indeed meet him in his inimitable suchness, and perhaps much more important, as would have been his hope, you will meet yourself.

JON KABAT-ZINN
Boston, Massachusetts

EDITOR'S PREFACE

Once upon a time in China, a young monk came to greet the master. After receiving his three full bows, the master asked: "Where have you come from?"

"From Seung Sahn [Exalted Mountain]," the young monk replied.

"Yes, but what is it that comes from Seung Sahn Mountain?"

The monk said, "If you call it a thing, it is already mistaken."

The master approved.

Naming is a mistake. Calling it anything is a mistake. Opening your mouth to say it is a mistake. Nowadays if you try to even draw it, it's a mistake—perhaps fatal. Some will riot and rampage to protest this mistake. Others believe just as strongly in the right to make this "mistake."

Both a mistake. Mistake, mistake, mistake. This book is about the mistake. That is also a very big mistake.

Several years ago, we received news from the good people at Shambhala Publications that the shipper would soon be delivering the first copies of a recently completed book by Zen Master Seung Sahn to the Zen center. We were all very excited, not least this editor, since I had spent some four years assembling the text from literally hundreds of shards of teachings and far-flung audio recordings, phrases he spoke that I had scratched onto crumpled envelope-backs. Now the text was finally arriving! Within a week, I was on a plane for a scheduled trip back to Korea, and would be able to hand the text directly to my teacher.

Arriving at his room in Hwa Gye Sah Temple, in the piney mountains above Seoul, I performed three full bows in kasa and formal robes. And reaching into a bag, pulled out the new book. I literally trembled with excitement to know that now there would be a full and meticulous statement of his teachings in English, as he once wished, and that now it was in his hands. How would he react? What would he say?

He fanned the book once slowly through his hand, its pages flying out from under his thumb too quickly to provide any time for taking in the matter on the pages within. You could feel the breeze of the pages from across the little writing table on which he was leaning. He may have stopped once to notice the Chinese characters accompanying one of the pages. If that. But I doubt it.

His disinterest seemed total. Not like the fantasy of getting a good back-clapping from the Master, or even a stern and Zen-masterly grunt or half-nod. Four long years sometimes picturing something that, now, wasn't going to happen. And then those words . . .

"Throw this book in the garbage," he said, waving it limply in the direction of a distant garbage pail. It wagged lifelessly from his fingers like a suddenly unnecessary fish. "Throw into garbage."

"Sir? Some mistake?"

"Many people will read these words, and become attached to them. So these words are number-one poison words.

Demon speech. That is a big mistake. Therefore, it would be better now to throw this book right into the garbage."

In a moment, the ego-driven disappointment gave way to extraordinary joy. His nonattachment even to his own teaching showed me how attached I was to my years of "hard" work putting it into book form. Stupid mistake.

So this book is already a big mistake, as he taught. "Don't want anything. Don't make anything. Don't hold anything. Don't attach to anything." And the greatest of these was "wanting," because this is where the whole infernal chain began.

Wanting enlightenment is a big mistake. It is a phrase he uttered not a few times, depending upon the question. In the Diamond Sutra, the Buddha asks Subhuti, "When I got supreme unexcelled enlightenment, what did I get? Did I get supreme unexcelled enlightenment?"

"No, Teacher," Subhuti replied. "You did not get anything when you got supreme unexcelled enlightenment."

"Correct," the Buddha continued. "Because if I had gotten anything, it would not be supreme unexcelled enlightenment."

This is what he was pointing to when Zen Master Seung Sahn taught, "You are already complete. You just don't know it." To *want* enlightenment is already a big mistake. Just *do* it.

Zen Master Seung Sahn passed from this world on November 30, 2004. This is the first compilation of his teachings to appear in English since his death. It contains excerpts from dialogues with students, interviews, and some of his own recounting of sections of his life translated for the first time from Korean.

What is more, this text contains a very important letter that he wrote to Chun Du-Hwan, the feared military strongman who came to power in a coup d'état and ruled South

Korea with an iron fist for much of the 1980s. This letter has never been published before, and only a few people outside of a handful of his closest students have even heard of the letter's existence, much less read it. I have retranslated the letter from its Korean original while consulting closely a contemporary translation.

This two-hundred-some-odd page mistake began as my master's thesis at the Harvard Divinity School, and submitted to the late Professor Masatoshi Nagatomi in April 1992. Shortly after I ordained, in September 1992, I showed it to Zen Master Seung Sahn. He said, "Make book necessary," and then complained of its thinness. It was circulated informally among several of the monks of the Kwan Um School of Zen, and eventually some of the material found its way into periodical newsletters of the Kwan Um School of Zen.

Eden Steinberg of Shambhala Publications encouraged this raw material to become a book. I thank her, Ben Gleason, and everyone at Shambhala for their high professionalism and wide-minded, generous handling of this teaching. Dr. Jon Kabat-Zinn and Joan Halifax, Roshi—both early students of Zen Master Seung Sahn—have contributed handsomely to this project, and the sangha thanks them. I also wish to express the deepest appreciation for the teaching and assistance of Zen Master Soeng Hyang (Barbara Rhodes), Zen Master Dae Kwang, Zen Master Dae Bong, and Zen Master Dae Kwan, all of the Kwan Um School of Zen.

HYON GAK SUNIM
Neung In Zen Center,
Jeong Hae Sah Temple
Dok Seung Sahn Mountain

WANTING ENLIGHTENMENT
IS A BIG MISTAKE

Enlightenment

A STUDENT HAD THE FOLLOWING exchange with Zen Master Seung Sahn:

"What is enlightenment?"

"Enlightenment is only a name," he replied. "If you make 'enlightenment,' then enlightenment exists. But if enlightenment exists, then ignorance exists, too. And that already makes an opposites-world. Good and bad, right and wrong, enlightened and ignorant—all of these are opposites. All opposites are just your own thinking. But truth is absolute, and is *before* any thinking or opposites appear. So if you make something, you will get something, and that something will be a hindrance. But if you don't make anything, you will get everything, OK?"

The student continued, "But is enlightenment really just a name? Doesn't a Zen master have to attain the experience of enlightenment in order to become a Zen master?"

"The *Heart Sutra* says that there is 'no attainment, with nothing to attain.' If enlightenment is attained, it is not true enlightenment. Having enlightenment is already a big mistake."

"Then is everyone already enlightened?"

Dae Soen Sa Nim* laughed and said, "Do you understand 'no attainment' "?

"No."

" 'No attainment' is true attainment. So I already told you about the *Heart Sutra*. It says, 'There is no attainment, with nothing to attain.' You must *attain* 'no attainment.' "

The student rubbed his head. "I think I understand . . ."

"You understand? So I ask you, what is attainment? What is there to attain?"

"Emptiness," the man replied.

"Emptiness?" Dae Soen Sa Nim asked. "But in true emptiness, there is no name and no form. So there is also no attainment. Even opening your mouth to express it, you are already mistaken. If you say, 'I have attained true emptiness,' you are wrong."

"Hmmm," the student said. "I'm beginning to understand. At least I think I am."

"The universe is always true emptiness, OK? Now you are living in a dream. Wake up! Then you will soon understand."

"How can I wake up?"

"I hit you!" (Laughter from the audience.) "Very easy, yah?"

The student was silent for a few moments, while Dae Soen Sa Nim eyed him intently. "I still don't get it. Would you please explain a bit more?"

"OK. Can you see your eyes?"

Dae Soen Sa Nim, meaning "Great Honored Zen Master," is the title by which Zen Master Seung Sahn's students refer to him in the West.

"Yes, I can."

"Oh? How?"

"By looking in a mirror."

"That's not your eyes! That is only a reflection of your eyes. So your eyes cannot see your eyes. If you try to see your eyes, it's already a big mistake. Talking about enlightenment is also like that. It's like your eyes trying to see your eyes."

"But my question is, when you were a young monk, you had the actual *experience* of enlightenment. What was this experience?"

"I hit you! Ha ha ha ha!"

The student was silent.

"OK, one more try. Suppose we have before us some honey, some sugar, and a banana. All of them are sweet. Can you explain the difference between honey's sweetness, sugar's sweetness, and banana's sweetness?"

"Hmmm . . ."

"But each has a different sweetness, yah? How can you explain it to me?"

The student looked suddenly even more perplexed. "I don't know . . ."

The Zen master continued, "Well, you could say to me, 'Open your mouth. *This* is honey, *this* is sugar, and *this* is banana!' Ha ha ha ha! So if you want to understand enlightenment, it's already making something. Don't make anything. Moment to moment, just *do* it. That's already enlightenment. So, first understand your true self. To understand your true self, you must understand the meaning of my hitting you. I have already put enlightenment into your mind. Ha ha ha ha! (Extended laughter from the audience)

The Rice-Pot Master

In the rolling countryside of old Korea, people used to gather from far and wide for big markets that lasted several days. The tradition continues until today. Everything imaginable can be found there, from common tools and cooking utensils to highly prized, hundred-year-old ginseng roots and baying livestock.

One hot summer day many years ago, a young man went to the market to sell the vegetables he had grown on his farm, and to use the money to buy rice. As he concluded his business with the rice seller, he noticed an old monk nearby, standing completely motionless in the blazing sun. The monk was wearing heavy winter clothes, tattered and worn, the stuffing bursting out from under old patches. Everyone else in the market had sought shade under trees or the eaves of the merchants' stalls. Many eyed the strange monk with aversion. But this old monk did not seem to care. He just stood there in the scorching sun, not moving at all.

"What is he, crazy?" the young man thought to himself. "Has he lost his mind? He's going to faint very soon." But despite the pounding heat, the monk did not move from his position. He even seemed to be smiling a little bit under his wide straw hat.

Later, after the young man had finished with other business, he approached the monk, who had just started to walk around with slow, gentle steps. "Sunim, Sunim!" ("Venerable monk!" "Venerable monk!") the man called, holding his hat in his hands and motioning to the cool of a nearby tree. "Excuse me, but why are you standing out in the sun like that? Shouldn't you be sitting in the shade?"

But the old monk did not answer right away. He only smiled at the young man kindly for a moment. "Lunch time," he said, in a voice so soft it was almost indiscernible.

"Lunch time?" The young man looked around. "It's already way past time. Who's eating?"

The monk opened his robe slightly, showing its puffy inside lining. All throughout the fabric, there were thousands of tiny insects, like lice, moving about in the heavy folds. "If I move too much, they cannot eat," the old monk said. "So sometimes I must only stand still while they have their lunch."

The young man immediately suspected the monk was deranged. But when he looked into the old monk's face, in his eyes there was no humor or strangeness, only compassion. The monk had very calm, clear eyes and relaxed features. His razor-stubbled features seemed to radiate a soft compassion.

"But why be so kind to such little creatures?"

The monk's eyes squinted easily, and he said, "Don't they value their lives just as dearly as you and I do?"

Deeply struck with the monk's extraordinary compassion, the young man immediately put his palms together politely, and bowed deeply to the monk. He asked if he could become the monk's student.

The monk shook his head and, smiling just as politely as before, said, "Not possible."

"Why isn't it possible?"

"Why do you want to become a monk?"

"I don't want to get married," the young man replied. "I want to find the correct way, and attain my true self. You are compassionate even to these tiny creatures. So I have a very strong feeling that maybe this is the correct way. You are a great monk, and I want to become your student."

"Maybe, maybe," said the monk. "But a monk's life is very difficult." He removed his hat and wiped his brow. "Where do you live?"

"My parents are dead, so I'm staying with my brother in the next village. I have no place of my own. I want to come with you."

"OK, let's go, then."

They walked straight up into the mountains, and did not stop for a long time. The old monk did not say anything as they wended their way deep into the mountain valleys. Past rolling streams and over rock walls, stopping only to rest silently together, after several hours of vigorous walking, they finally reached a small mud and stone house.

In Korea, kitchens are kept apart from the house. In every kitchen is a big black kettle, on a low stand, and a fire is lit under it. The pot is made of iron, and is very, very heavy. In this house, both pot and stand were broken. Fixing the pot requires a lot of heavy work. It also means pouring a little water into the pot to make sure that it settles evenly in the middle of the rounded bottom. If water does not settle evenly, then any food that is cooked there will cook poorly, and be wasted. It is very difficult work to adjust one of these kettles.

Pointing at the kettle, the monk uttered his first words since leaving the market together. "Please fix this." And just as suddenly, he left the kitchen.

The young man was only too eager to begin. Dismantling the old arrangement, he planed, graded, and resurfaced the setting where the kettle fits over the fire. When he had finished, he brought the monk over. "It is all fixed."

The old monk checked it, eyeing the edges and pouring in a ladleful of water. "No good!" he said, and dumped out the water. "Try again!"

The young man thought, "Hmmm, this monk has very keen eyes, so he must see some mistake." He tried to fix it again, this time being very careful to regrade and adjust every edge of the kettle. This time he ladled water into the kettle to check the level himself, and stood up from his work more satisfied than before. He brought the monk over. "Sir, now I have correctly fixed the pot."

"OK, I will check." The old monk squinted at the edges of the kettle, slowly ladling water down the sides. "No good!" he said, and dumped out the water. "Try again!"

The young man became very confused. "I must be making some mistake! Where is my mistake?" he thought to himself. He was very, very confused! "Perhaps it is outside the pot. Maybe the stand is not correct." This time, he prepared the pot very closely, scrutinizing every inch of it for flaws in the setting. Whatever he had even the slightest doubt about, he fixed completely. Then he checked the whole counter area, where the pot was situated, and made sure everything was clean and neat. He tested and retested the level with several ladles of water. Rubbing his tired back, he again went to fetch his teacher. "Sunim, I have fixed the pot! Everything has been checked twice over. Now I am sure you will like it."

"No good!" the monk said after examining the pot, and dumped out the water. "Again!"

The young man did not understand what was wrong. "This monk sees some mistake: why can't I? I know the pot is good," he thought. "Maybe the kitchen is no good." So he tore out the entire kitchen, every board of it, and rebuilt it completely, from floor to ceiling. "There," he said as he wiped his brow. "Sunim cannot help but approve of it now." So he went to fetch his teacher. "Sunim, I've fixed the whole kitchen! I am *sure* there is no mistake now! Please come and check."

"Oh, that's wonderful! You are working very hard, so I am very happy. Now I will check." He went to the pot, dumped in a ladle of water and, seeming almost as if he did not even take the time to see how level the water settled, he shouted, "No good!" and turned it over again.

This happened four times, five times, six, seven, eight times. Each time, the young man thought, "What's wrong with it this time?" and each time the monk answered, "Mistake! No good!" and dumped out the water.

By now, the young man was getting *very* angry! "Where is my mistake?" After the ninth time the water was dumped out, he said to himself, "This monk is not correct! I don't care what he says now. This is the last time!" So he just set the pot on the stand and called out, "Sunim, I am finished!" When the master came into the kitchen to see, the young man was sitting on the pot, arms folded across his chest.

"Wonderful! Wonderful!" cried the master, and trundled off to get his meal bowls. That night they ate rice and delicious soup together. The kettle was never mentioned again.

* * *

Zen Master Seung Sahn once commented on this story to his students as follows:

"This old monk was testing his student's mind. That is because Zen means not depending on anything. You must depend on yourself, whatever your own style is.

"But what is your own style? If you keep your opinions, your condition, and your situation, and hold your *I-my-me* mind, then your correct style cannot appear. So this monk had great compassion, and only tested his student's mind. 'This young man wants to become a monk. But how much does he believe in himself?' Each time the student fixed the pot, he thought, 'Maybe this will pass; maybe that will pass'—much thinking. His mind was easily moved. When the Zen monk dumped out the water, the student believed the monk when he said there was still something wrong with the pot, even when there was no problem. This was all just the teacher's way of testing the student's mind, and seeing how much the young man's mind moved. But the last time, the student just did it. There was no wavering, no self-doubt. His mind did not move in the least.

"The Zen monk was also testing his student's perseverance mind. 'This young man likes me, but how much does he want to understand his true self?' Usually, most people try maybe four or five times to match themselves against the teacher's wisdom. If the teacher doesn't approve very soon, many students will say, 'I don't like you!' and then go away. But when they say, 'I don't like you' or 'I don't like this teaching,' what they are really saying is that they don't like themselves. A good teacher only reflects the student's mind. If students don't like what they see, sometimes they blame it on their teacher.

"So a *try-mind* is more important than any Zen master. If you say, 'I can,' then you can do something. If you say, 'I cannot,' then you cannot do anything. Which one do you like?

"This is the reason why we say, 'Only go straight, try, try, try for ten thousand years, nonstop.' *Try, try, try* means persevere, from moment to moment. It is sometimes called Right Effort. It is the mind that always tries, no matter what, in any condition and any situation. That is already enlightenment. That is already saving all beings. That is already the Great Bodhisattva Way. So trying is very necessary. Then one day, maybe the Zen master will say to you, 'Oh, wonderful!'"

Not-Thinking Action

AFTER A DHARMA SPEECH at the Lithuania Zen Center, a student asked Zen Master Seung Sahn, "I know the Buddha taught that we shouldn't kill. But sometimes, when a mosquito lands on my arm, I slap and kill it. I don't plan it out or think about doing it. It just happens. This action kills a life, but does it violate the Buddha's teaching?"

Dae Soen Sa Nim replied, "This is a very important question. We can say that there are two kinds of action: thinking-action, and not-thinking action, which we also call *reflect-action*. Let's say you are driving a car, and somebody steps out onto the street, right in your path. If you pause, even for a tiny moment, and think, 'Oh my God! How will I avoid him?' or 'Stupid guy, why did he walk out into the street like that?' you will surely hit him. If you think, then somebody will die! The name for that is *thinking-action*. Thinking-action leaves some trace behind, some effect: we can call that a kind of karmic residue.

"But if you see this man step out onto the street, and in the moment of seeing, just hit the brake, you will not kill him.

You perceive and act all at once. It's like a mirror: if a red ball comes before the mirror, the mirror reflects red; when a white ball appears, white. There is no space, no thinking, no holding: only action. The name for that is *reflect-action,* which means just *do* it. Reflect-action means there is no 'my thinking,' so this action is beyond good and bad.

"But there is good reflect-action, and bad reflect-action. In Korea, there is a famous temple called Su Dok Sah. Many tourists come from all over the country to see it. The Main Buddha Hall is a very beautiful, ancient Dharma hall. It is a national treasure in Korea. Its doors are very large and heavy. Often when people open one of these doors, it gets caught by the wind and flies open. BAM!—the huge door slams into the wall. Most people are very careful with it, but if the wind is blowing, it can really fly open.

"One time a few years ago, a group of American Zen students were visiting Korea, so we went to visit Su Dok Sah Temple for the day. We went into this Main Buddha Hall, and I started to tell them about the history of Su Dok Sah Temple: you know, 'This temple is fourteen hundred years old. . . .' This kind of speech. Then while I was speaking, a very old Korean woman tried to get in, and pushed the door open a little too far. *Psshhhewww!!*—a sudden gust of wind caught it. The edge of the door flew out of her hands!

"But there was this one American Zen student standing several feet away, listening to my talk. Though he wasn't looking directly at the woman as she entered, he heard the door start to move and pick up speed. He just heard this sound of a creaking door, and—*psshhhewww!!*—he flew like an arrow, even between several people standing in the way, and grabbed the door just before it hit the wall. He saved the door of this big national treasure from breaking, so maybe he also saved that woman from suffering, too! (Laughter.) So this Zen student's no-thinking action helped other people's consciousness: he was not thinking good or bad, enough time or not enough time, 'Can I do it?' or 'Is there enough time?' His mind was only reflecting, like a mirror. That is a good example of reflect-action.

"I have one more story: During the Korean War, all Korean males of a certain age were required to enter the army—even monks! When I was in the army, I had a very good friend, Mr. Song. We always did together-action, together-action, together-action. Any time I had a little money, I would take him to a restaurant or we would visit a temple together. Every day, I only tried to help him, but he never had any money. That was no problem for me, but Mr. Song wanted to repay in some way. 'I am sorry, I am sorry,' he would say. 'I cannot take care of you!'

"One day, Mr. Song said, 'Oh, sir, today it's my turn. We're going to a wonderful high-class restaurant in Taegu City for lunch!'

"I said to him, 'But you don't have any money. How can you get enough money for that?' Especially during wartime, it was very difficult to get money for such things as eating in restaurants.

"He said, 'No problem, don't worry. I'll get some.' So we went to the Taegu City train station. It's a very big station, with many people coming and going. Mr. Song whistled very loudly, and suddenly three boys came running up to him. They all bowed to him and said, 'Oh, older brother, where have you come from?' He said, 'From Such-and-such City. Where are Mr. Lee and Mr. Kim? I want to talk with them.' The boys ran off, and within a few minutes two very well-dressed gentlemen appeared. 'Oh, older brother, you've come today! How nice to see you!' They were very happy, and very kind to my friend. They treated him with great formality and respect.

"Pointing to me, he said to them, 'This man is my very good friend. He helps me all the time. We've come to have lunch together. Can you prepare this lunch?'

"'Yes, brother,' they said. So the two men brought a car around and drove us to this very wonderful high-class restaurant. They served us certain foods that I had not eaten or even seen in years, due to the war. Meanwhile, I couldn't understand what was happening, because on top of this, my friend clearly had no money! But that didn't matter—we had very good food together, and Mr. Song was very happy, so I was happy, too. Very good feeling!

"After lunch, as Mr. Song leaned back, picking his teeth, I asked him, 'What is happening? How is this possible?'

"'Oh, it's a very long story,' he said.

"'Please tell me.'

"'OK. Before I went into the army, I was a top pickpocket. I was the boss, and those men were my attendants. One day, I realized that this was all very bad action. So I repented, washed my hands of it, and went into the army. But all the time you have been helping me out, and I haven't been able to repay you—I have no money. Today I returned the favor: some repentance was necessary, so I called my old friends.'

"Then I said, 'That kind of action is not correct! If you really washed your hands of it, then that means *no more*!!'

"'OK, OK. I won't do this anymore,' he said. 'I promise.' He had always been very correct in the army, and even became a captain. We were captains together, and I saw that his actions were always very meticulous and correct. So this pickpocketing was like an old habit.

"One day, we went sightseeing at Sorak Sahn Mountain, a

very beautiful and famous mountain in Korea. The weather was very nice. Many people come from all over to see this mountain, so there were a lot of people in the bus station when we arrived. Mr. Song was walking in front of me. There were many people waiting in lines. All of a sudden, Mr. Song's hand quickly went into the pocket of the man standing in front of us and took out his wallet! *Psshhhewww!!* It was like lightning! But I was standing right behind him, and saw this happen, so I hit him—BOOM! 'Your hand is no good!'

"He was very surprised. 'Oh, that's my old habit. I cannot help it. It just happens!' He was very sorry, and very sincere. He didn't want to take this wallet; he didn't want to be a pickpocket and take people's money anymore. But he saw a wallet and automatically his hand reached out and took it. That was his mind's old, strong habit.

"I told him, 'You must return that money!'

"'Yes, yes.' Then he tapped the shoulder of the man standing in front of him. 'Excuse me, sir. Is this your wallet? I found it on the floor.'

"The man turned and saw Mr. Song holding his wallet. 'Oh, yes, my money! Thank you, thank you! I was on my way to the market to buy a cow with this money. If I had lost it, I wouldn't have been able to buy the cow. Oh, thank you very much!' He took out some money to give to Mr. Song as a reward.

"'Oh no, no. I couldn't!' Mr. Song waved his hands in modest refusal.

"But I elbowed my friend in the side. 'It's OK to take a little. Now that's your job.' So Mr. Song took a little money. (Laughter.)

"These two stories show two kinds of no-thinking action, what we also call *reflect-action*. The young American Zen student's action, darting for the door at Su Dok Sah Temple, was without thinking, like a good habit that only helps others and does not think of oneself. Such an action does not leave anything behind in the mind, because it functions from empty mind, just like a mirror. When something is reflected in the mirror, it is reflected. When it leaves the face of the mirror, there is no longer any reflection. The mirror does not hold anything. We call this *reflect-mind.* Because it doesn't depend on thinking, it does not make karma.

"My pickpocket friend, Mr. Song, had a kind of reflect-mind, but more on the order of a bad habit: sometimes even without thinking, his hand reached for wallets. But he reflected off of his desire, his old habit to desire someone else's money. Thinking makes a habit, and a habit makes more thinking: this is karma. This kind of action produces karma.

"Everyone has good and bad habits. That is no problem. Only keep a clear mind, clear mind, clear mind, moment to moment, and then a correct habit will appear by itself. That, we say, is *correct* karma—it is not good karma or bad karma. It is beyond good and bad. The sky is blue: is that good or bad? That is beyond good and bad, yah? Water is flowing: is that good or bad? That, too, is beyond good and bad.

"Good and bad do not matter—they are only names. If you only do good actions, then when you die you'll go to heaven; do bad actions, and go to hell.

"But if you keep a clear mind, moment to moment, then only correct actions appear, and you are not hindered by heaven or hell. That is the meaning of Bodhisattva action, which is for the good of all beings and is beyond life and death. The most important matter to be clear about is *why* do you do something: only for yourself, or for all beings? If you find that, then any action is no problem. That's a very important point. That is Zen practicing and Zen direction."

Shoot the Buddha!

AFTER A DHARMA TALK at the Cambridge Zen Center, a young woman said to Zen Master Seung Sahn, "Tomorrow is my son's birthday, and he told me he wants either a toy gun or money. But I have a problem: As a Zen student, I want to teach him not to hurt or crave things. So I don't want to give him a toy gun or money. What should I do?"

Dae Soen Sa Nim replied, "That's very easy: buy him the toy gun! (Laughter from the audience.) If you give him money, he will only go out and buy a toy gun. (Laughter.) Today a few of us went to see a movie called *Cobra*, starring Sylvester Stallone. Do you know this movie? A very simple story: good guy versus bad guys. Other movies are very complicated, you know? But this movie had only two things: bad and good. Bad. Good. A very simple story.

"Your son wants a toy gun. You think that that is not so good. But instead, you should view the problem as how do you *use* this correctly? Don't make good or bad: how do you teach the correct *function* of this gun, OK? That's very important—more important than just having a gun or not is having

17

the wisdom to perceive the gun's correct function. If you use this gun correctly, you can help many people, but if it is not used correctly, then maybe you will kill yourself, kill your country, kill other people. So the gun itself is originally not good, not bad. More important is: what is the correct *function* of this gun?

"So you must teach your son: if Buddha appears, kill!! If the eminent teachers appear, kill!! If a Zen master appears, you must kill!! If demons appear, kill! This is another way of saying that if anything appears in your mind you must kill anything, OK? (Laughter.) Then you will become Buddha! (Much laughter.) So you must teach your son in this way. The gun itself is not good or bad, good or bad. These are only names. Most important is *why* do you do or use something: is it only for 'me,' or for all beings? That is the most important point to consider."

Why Zen Seems Difficult

AFTER A DHARMA TALK at the Cambridge Zen Center, someone asked Zen Master Seung Sahn, "Why does Zen seem so difficult?"

"Difficult?"

"Yes," the man said. "Why does it *seem* so difficult? I didn't say it *was,* but why does it seem so difficult?"

"Seem difficult? Zen is very easy: why make 'difficult?'"

The man persisted, "All right, I'll ask you as a psychologist: why do I make it difficult?"

"A psychologist said that? Who said what?"

"Why do I or anybody make Zen difficult?"

"You say 'difficult,' so it's difficult. A long time ago in China lived a famous man named Layman Pang. His whole family was a Zen family. Layman Pang used to be rich, but then he realized that many people don't have enough food to eat. So he gave all of his land to the farmers. He had many precious jewels and other possessions, but he thought, 'If I give things away, they'll only create desire-mind in other people.' So he took a boat out to the middle of a very deep lake and

19

dumped all his priceless possessions overboard. Then he and his son went and lived in a cave; meanwhile, his wife and daughter moved into a very small house. Sometimes the Pangs would visit Zen temples to have Dharma combat with the monks. They had a very simple life, and practiced very hard.

"One day, someone asked Layman Pang, 'Is Zen difficult or easy?'

"He replied, 'It's like trying to hit the moon with a stick. Very difficult!'

"Then this man thought, 'Oh, Zen is very difficult.' So he asked Layman Pang's wife, 'Your husband said Zen is difficult. I ask you, then, is Zen difficult or easy?'

"She said, 'Oh, Zen is very easy! It's like touching your nose when you wash your face in the morning!'

"The man could not understand. He thought to himself, 'Hmmm . . . . Layman Pang says Zen is difficult; his wife says it is very easy. Which one is correct?' So he went to their son and said, 'Your father said Zen is very difficult; your mother said it is very easy. Which one is correct?'

"The son replied, 'If you think it's difficult, then it's difficult. If you think it's easy, then it's easy. Don't make difficult and easy!'

"But the man was still not satisfied, so he went to the daughter. 'Everyone in your whole family has a different answer to my question. Your mother said Zen is easy. Your father said Zen is difficult. And your brother said don't make difficult and easy. So I ask you, is Zen difficult or easy?'

" 'Go drink tea.' "

Dae Soen Sa Niim looked at the student who asked the question and said, "So, go drink tea, OK? Don't make 'difficult.' Don't make 'easy.' Don't make anything. From moment to moment, just *do* it!"

Crazy Mind

AFTER A DHARMA TALK at the Cambridge Zen Center, a student asked Zen Master Seung Sahn, "Is there such a thing as a clean mind?"

"If you have mind, then you must clean your mind. If you have no mind, cleaning is not necessary. So I ask you, do you have a mind?"

"Do I?"

"Do you?"

"Yes, I do."

"Where is it?"

The student looked puzzled for a moment. "Where *is* it?"

"Yes, where is it? How big is your mind?"

"Uhhh . . ."

"This much (holding arms open wide) or this much (narrowing them together)?"

The student tilted his head back and stretched his arms open wide. "This much right now."

"Ooohh, only that? That's very small! Not even as big as this room, it seems. (Much laughter from the assembly.)

That's not your original mind. Originally, your mind is the whole universe; the whole universe and your mind are the same. Why do you make just 'this much'? So that is a problem. Since you make 'this-much' mind, now you must dry-clean your mind. Use *don't-know* soap. If you clean, clean, clean your mind, it will become bigger, bigger, and bigger—as big as the whole universe. But if there is any taint, it becomes smaller, smaller, smaller. But actually, you have no mind, I think."

"You think I have no mind?"

"Yes, no mind."

The student was silent.

"You don't understand, yah? Do you have mind?"

"Well, I don't understand a lot of . . . I don't understand a lot . . . umm . . . I . . .." (Laughter.)

"The Sixth Patriarch said, 'Originally nothing: where can dust alight?' So maybe you have no mind."

After a long silence, the student brightened a bit. "OK, you talk about Right Livelihood, you talk about having monk karma and wanting to practice Zen . . . umm . . . and my question is . . . not to live in a Zen center . . . to live in the world it's very difficult to practice, umm . . . to connect practice and livelihood, umm . . . So the mind that meets the mind that's conflicted is the mind I'm speaking with . . . from . . . umm . . ."

"Yah, your mind is a strange mind," Dae Soen Sa Nim said.

"A strange mind?"

"Yah, strange mind. Nowadays everybody has a strange mind, because inside it's not correct, not meticulous, not clear. This strange mind is like an animal's mind, not really a human being's mind. It is maybe 80 percent animal mind,

20 percent human mind. So that is strange, that's crazy, and considered normal. Nowadays there are many, many crazy people. But everybody is crazy, so this crazy is not special. Even a Zen master's speech is crazy. Yesterday I said in a Dharma speech, 'The sun rises in the east and sets in the west.' Those are crazy words. The sun never rises in the east nor sets in the west. The sun never moves! Only the earth moves, around and around the sun, so why make this speech about the sun rising in the east and setting in the west? That's crazy! (Laughter.) So that means: crazy is not crazy. Not crazy is crazy. (He looks at the questioner's face.) Do you understand that? Crazy is not crazy; not crazy is crazy."

The student starts to say something, but stops.

"Ha, ha, ha! Now your thinking is complicated! That's no problem. Zen teaches that if you have mind, you have a problem. If you don't have mind, then everything is no hindrance. But everybody makes mind, so there are many problems in this world. Say you own a hotel. Mind is like this hotel's manager, who should be working for you. Usually, everything is OK in the hotel, but this manager is always causing problems: 'I want this, I want that.' 'I like this, I don't like that.' 'I want to be free, go here, do that . . .' That is mind, OK? The Buddha taught, 'When mind appears, dharma appears. When dharma appears, form appears. When form appears, then like/dislike, coming/going, life and death, everything appears.' So if you have mind, you have a problem; no mind, no problem. Here are some very popular words: 'Everything is created by mind alone.' These are good words; they have a good taste. Your mind makes something, and something hinders you. So don't make anything! Take your mind and throw it into the garbage. Only don't *know*!"

The student merely sat expressionless, staring at the floor.

"So Zen practice means you fire this low-class hotel manager because he's doing a bad job in your high-class hotel. You must take control of your hotel, which means you control your eyes, ears, nose, tongue, body, and mind. The owner must be strong. If the manager doesn't do his job correctly, the owner must say, 'You are no good!! Why didn't you fix these things?! That's your job! Why did you take all the money?! I'm going to fire you!' Then this manager will be afraid, 'Oh, please don't fire me! Please!' Then the owner must say, 'You listen to me, OK?' 'OK, OK, I'll only follow you from now on!'

"You must hit your mind, OK? Tell your mind, 'You must listen to *me*!' If your mind says 'OK,' then no problem. If not, you must cut this mind. How? You must use your don't-know sword. Always hold on to this don't-know sword: mind is very afraid of it. If you keep this don't-know sword, then everything is no problem."

Brightening up considerably, the student bowed and said, "Thank you very much for your teaching."

Zen Master Ko Bong's Try-Mind

Zen Master Seung Sahn's teacher, Zen Master Ko Bong, was one of the greatest teachers of his time. He was renowned for refusing to teach many monks, calling them lazy and arrogant Zen students. He was also very well known for his wild, unpredictable behavior.

One day when he was a young monk, Ko Bong Sunim was traveling in the mountains. He stopped at a small temple along the way and decided to stay there for a week. After a few days, the abbot of the temple went to visit the home of a student, so Ko Bong Sunim was the only one left in the temple. Later that afternoon, an old woman climbed the steep road to the temple where Ko Bong Sunim was staying, carrying fruit and a bag of rice on her back. When she reached the Main Buddha Hall, she found Ko Bong Sunim, seated in meditation.

"Oh, Sunim, I am sorry," she said. "I have just climbed this mountain to offer these things to the Buddha. There are many problems in my family, and I want someone to chant to the Buddha for me. Can you please help me?" Her face was very sad, and also very sincere.

Ko Bong Sunim looked up at her. "Of course," he said. "I'd be happy to chant for you. No problem." But Ko Bong Sunim didn't know the first thing about performing ceremonies. Though he had been a monk for several years, he had lived in a Zen temple, where the monks only sit Zen. In Korea, there are ceremony monks who chant for ceremonies, sutra (scripture) monks who study the sutras, and Zen monks, who just sit. So Ko Bong Sunim didn't know anything about what traditional chants to do, or even how to do them; he didn't know how to hit the *moktak** or when to bow at the appropriate time. But he thought to himself, "No problem, no problem. Only do it. OK. No problem—only do it."

Ko Bong Sunim put his formal robes on. Because he had never led a ceremony on his own before, he didn't know the appropriate Buddhist chants. Usually, it is appropriate to do certain chants for different occasions, like the *Thousand Eyes and Hands Sutra,* but Ko Bong Sunim didn't know about this. He did remember some old Taoist scripture that he had read years ago, before becoming a monk. So he banged the *moktak* and chanted the Taoist scripture out loud, bowing from time to time, whenever he felt the whim. He just made it up as he went along. After an hour or so of this, he finished.

The old woman was very, very happy. "Oh, thank you, Sunim. You are very kind. I feel much better now!" she said, and she left the temple. As she was walking down the mountain road, she passed the abbot, who was returning from his visit. "Hello Mrs. So-and-so, are you coming from the temple?"

"Yes," she said. "There are many problems in my family right now, so I went up to pray to the Buddha. Ko Bong Sunim helped me."

*A carved wooden instrument struck rhythmically to pace Buddhist chanting.

"Oh, that's too bad," the abbot said.

"Oh, why?"

"Because Ko Bong Sunim doesn't know how to do this kind of chanting. Maybe someone else could—"

"No, no," she said. "He did *very* well. He helped me very much!"

The abbot looked at her. "How do you know how well he did? These are very special chants! Ko Bong Sunim is a meditation monk; he doesn't know how to do any of them—he doesn't know correct chanting."

"Yes, I understand." This woman used to be a nun, so she was quite familiar with all the various chants. She knew that Ko Bong Sunim was only chanting a Taoist scripture. "What is correct chanting? What is not correct chanting? He did it very well. He chanted 100 percent. Words are not important— only how you keep your mind is important. He had only try-mind."

"Oh, yes, yes! Of course, of course!" the abbot said. "I suppose mind is very important." They said goodbye and went their separate ways. When the abbot reached the temple, he found Ko Bong Sunim seated in meditation. "Did you just chant for Mrs. So-and-so?"

"Yes."

"But you don't know anything about chanting."

"That's right," Ko Bong Sunim said. "I don't know anything about chanting. So I just chanted."

"Then, what kind of chants did you do?" the abbot asked.

"I used some old Taoist text. It was very wonderful."

The abbot walked away, scratching his head.

This is a very interesting try-mind story. It means, from moment to moment, only *do* it. Only keep a try-mind, only one mind: only *do-it* mind. When chanting, or sitting, or bowing, even special practicing cannot help you if you are attached to your thinking. Taoist chanting, Confucian chanting, Christian chanting, Buddhist chanting don't matter. Chanting "Coca Cola, Coca Cola, Coca Cola . . ." can be just as good if you keep a clear mind. But if you don't keep a clear mind, and are only following your thinking as you mouth the words, even the Buddha cannot help you. The most important thing is, only *do* it. When you only do something, 100 percent, then there is no subject and no object. There's no inside or outside. Inside and outside already become one. That means you and the universe are never separate. There is no thinking.

The Bible says, "Be still, and know that I am God." When you become still, then you don't make anything, and you are always connected to God. *Being still* means keeping a still mind, even if your body is moving or doing some activity. Then there's no subject, no object: a mind of perfect stillness. That is the Buddha's complete-stillness mind. When sitting, be still. When chanting, be still. When bowing, eating, talking, walking, reading, or driving, only be still. This is keeping a not-moving mind, which is an only do-it mind. The name for that is *try-mind*.

Frog Stand

ZEN MASTER SEUNG SAHN'S GREAT-GRANDTEACHER, Zen Master Kyong Ho, is one of the most renowned Zen teachers in Korean history. One day, many years ago, he went for a walk in the countryside with his student, Yong Song Sunim, who was known for being very kind and gentle about everything he did. As they passed a small pond, they noticed that a group of young boys had set up a table by the side of the road. This table was like a lemonade stand, but different in one respect: the boys had caught many, many frogs, tied string around their hind legs, and tethered them to the ground. Passersby would buy some of these frogs, take them home, fry them over a fire, and eat them.

Seeing the frog stand from the road, Yong Song Sunim stopped. "Teacher, please have a little rest. I'll be right back," he said. Then he approached the young boys. "I'd like to buy all of those frogs," he said, taking a few coins out of his pocket. "Here is some money." So they sold him all the frogs. The boys jumped up and down with glee! They were very, very happy as they pocketed the money and skipped away, dragging their traps and lures.

Then Yong Song Sunim untied the string from the frogs and tossed the frogs back into the pond—*pluke! pluke! pluke!*—one by one. The frogs were very happy, kicking their way back and forth through the water. Yong Song Sunim was happy, too, as he watched them contentedly, a big smile spreading across his face.

Dusting off his hands, and grinning proudly to himself, Yong Song Sunim walked back to the road, where Zen Master Kyong Ho was fanning himself gently with his straw monk's hat in the shade of a tree. Yong Song Sunim said, "Glad we came by this way. I just saved all those frogs."

"That is very wonderful," Kyong Ho Sunim said. "But you're going to go to hell."

Yong Song Sunim was very startled at this. "Why will I go to hell? I just freed those frogs!"

"Yes, you freed those frogs. And you're going straight to hell like an arrow," Kyong Ho Sunim said.

"Why will I go to hell?"

"You already understand!"

"No, Teacher, I do not," Yong Song Sunim said. "Please teach me."

"You say 'I' saved those frogs. You make 'I,' but this 'I' does not exist. Making this 'I' is already a big mistake. If you keep that I-my-me mind, then even though you do some great action that impresses many people, you go directly to hell."

Yong Song Sunim bowed deeply. "Oh, Teacher, thank you very much for your teaching."

Zen Master Man Gong's Thumb-and-Forefinger Zen

MANY YEARS AGO, a reporter from a prominent Seoul daily newspaper decided to do a story on Zen Master Man Gong. This Zen master was known throughout the country for his strong and clear teaching style. He also taught Zen to nuns and laypeople, which was very unusual in those days. When the occupying Japanese tried to take total control of Buddhist practice in Korea in the 1940s, Zen Master Man Gong refused to cooperate, risking his life even to the point of challenging the all-powerful Japanese colonial governor himself. So because of these things, but above all for his deeply enlightened mind and extraordinary energy, his reputation spread far and wide. When the newspaper reporter heard that some three hundred monks, nuns, and laypeople had gathered around a temple, Su Dok Sah Temple, to practice under Zen Master Man Gong, he decided to go there for his story. With pencil and paper in hand, he set out for the temple.

In those days, Zen Master Man Gong was living in a tiny

hermitage near the top of Dok Sahn Mountain. It was agreed that the great Zen master would descend to Jeong Hae Sah Temple, the meditation hall located midway up the mountain, at the base of which is Su Dok Sah Temple. Before going up to see the Zen master, the reporter met some friends who were staying down at Su Dok Sah Temple. "I'm going up to see Zen Master Man Gong," he said to them. "I'm going to interview him for a story."

"Oh, that's very wonderful," said one friend. "You are *very* lucky."

Another piped in, "Be careful! They say he is like a ferocious lion. I wouldn't want to be left alone with him for too long!" Undaunted, the reporter left his friends and started up the mountain. Midway up, he reached Jeong Hae Sah Temple, and received permission to enter Zen Master Man Gong's room.

Zen Master Man Gong was sitting in the center of the room. The reporter took out his pencil and paper and sat down facing him. "How are you, great Zen Master?" he asked.

Man Gong Sunim simply nodded once without saying anything.

"Uhh . . . I've come from Seoul, and . . ."

Man Gong Sunim didn't say a word.

"I work for Such-and-such newspaper there, and . . ."

Still silent. This made the reporter feel a little more nervous.

"Well, let's get to the point," the reporter said. "What is Buddhism?"

Man Gong Sunim held up his hand, touching thumb and forefinger together to form a circle.

The reporter thought that perhaps the Zen master was

hard of hearing, so he asked again, "What is Buddhism? What does Buddhism *teach*?"

Man Gong Sunim made the same gesture.

"I . . . I . . . don't think you understand," he persisted. "I'm trying to find out what *Buddhism* is about."

Man Gong Sunim made the same gesture.

"I . . . I . . . don't think you understand," he persisted. "I'm trying to find out . . . to hear your explanation . . . what Buddhism is about . . ."

Again, Man Gong Sunim made the same gesture.

The reporter couldn't understand, and worst of all, he couldn't write anything down because the Zen master wasn't saying anything!

In Korea, gesturing with thumb and forefinger in a circle is sometimes used to connote "money." "Hmmm . . . maybe he wants a donation," he thought to himself, and reached into his pocket. He proffered a few coins.

Man Gong Sunim still said nothing.

"Maybe he's sick," he thought. But Man Gong Sunim gave no other response. After a few more minutes of this, a silence broken here and there by the sound of birds chirping merrily outside the hut, the reporter took his pencil and pad and headed back down the mountain. When he reached the bottom, he found his friends. "What is so special about that old monk? I asked him, 'What is Buddhism?' and he only went like this. I think he meant 'coin.' Does he need any money?"

His friends laughed at him. "The monks at Jeong Hae Sah Temple have studied with the old master for many years. Why don't you go back up there and ask the head monk what his teacher meant?"

"Oh, good idea," the reporter said. So he puffed his way

back up the mountain and found the head monk at Jeong Hae Sah Temple. "Sunim, I asked your teacher what Buddhism is about, and he only made this gesture. What does this mean?"

The head monk opened his mouth wide and chomped his teeth together three times. The newspaperman was completely bewildered. "This head monk is crazier than the master!" he thought to himself. So he went back down the mountain and told his friends what had happened with the head monk. The whole experience completely flustered him!

One of the men laughed out loud at his friend's knotted face, and said, "Zen Master Man Gong has already explained everything perfectly to you. It's very, very clear. If you understood your true self, you'd understand what he meant."

But this did not satisfy the reporter. He went back to Seoul and wrote the article as best he could, given the lack of notes. All he could say was, "I couldn't understand Zen Master Man Gong. I couldn't understand the head monk at Jeong Hae Sah Temple. My friends at Su Dok Sah Temple told me I'd first have to understand my true nature if I wanted to understand this great Zen master. Buddhism seems more a mystery to me than ever!"

Many people read this article, and were interested by the Zen master's answer. So even more people than before began to flock to Jeong Hae Sah Temple. One woman prominent in Seoul intellectual circles also read the article. The Zen master's answer deeply pierced her mind. She had been having many problems with the way women were treated in this traditional Confucian society, and struggled with men because of it. But fighting did not help her. "Why are things like this? What is man; what is woman? What is truth? I don't understand." Then she read the article about the Zen master and his seemingly meaningless answer, and her mind became completely stuck. That very day, the woman went to see Zen Master Man Gong.

When she finally was able to obtain a meeting with the Zen master, she instantly began a barrage of questions: "What is truth? Why is there suffering? What's my correct way?"

But Man Gong Sunim cut her off. "If you open your mouth, you've already missed it. You've got two eyes, two ears, and two nostrils—how come only one mouth? If you had another one in the back of your head, you would be able to eat with one and go on talking with the other at the same time. Why do you have only one mouth?"

The woman was silent, and could not answer. She was completely stuck. "I don't know . . . I . . . I . . ." All of her many questions suddenly became this one big question.

"First you must understand why you have only one mouth. Then you will understand the truth."

So the woman cut her hair and became a nun. She practiced meditation very, very diligently: "What am I? What am I?" After long efforts, her mind shot open. Zen Master Man Gong tested her realization, and gave her *inka*.* Years later, she wrote many books and became quite famous throughout Korea. But only after she understood why she had just one mouth. That was Zen Master Man Gong's thumb-and-forefinger teaching to her.

Inka is a teacher's formal recognition of a student's realization, or breakthrough in practice.

Original Clothes

ZEN MASTER SEUNG SAHN was known as a spontaneous, wide-minded teacher with a view as vast and deep as the universe. Whether it was owing to this or not, many Zen students who came to him for *kong-an* interviews attempted to express their insight into Zen through strange or unorthodox actions, believing that this alone would impress him.*

One day, while giving formal *kong-an* interviews during a seven-day retreat at the Cambridge Zen Center, a student entered the room completely naked, bowed, and sat down facing Zen Master Seung Sahn.

"Good morning!" Dae Soen Sa Nim said, completely nonplussed by the student's obvious attempt to shock him with this strange behavior.

---

*A *kong-an* (Jap. *koan*), one of the least understood aspects of Zen training, is a question given to Zen students to deepen and clarify their existential doubt, leading to enlightenment. Seemingly paradoxical in nature, a *kong-an* cannot be unlocked through rational thought. Its truest expression must burst out of the student's deepest innermost being, and is often expressed through sounds or actions, which, however meaningless to a casual observer, can reveal to an enlightened teacher the true depth of a student's realization in meditation and life.

"Good morning, Zen Master," the student replied.

"So, I ask you, where are you coming from?"

The student stood up and waved his hips around, saying, "WO, WO, WO!!" In response to a request from this student, who had had trouble letting go of his thoughts during meditation, Seung Sahn Sunim had, as a teaching expedient, taught him this sound several years previous, saying, "Just keep this universal sound."

"Very interesting!" Seung Sahn Sunim laughed, and then asked in a stern voice, "But is that really correct?"

The student kept waving his hips: "WO, WO, WO!!"

"Ah, you only understand One; but you don't understand two. You only understand this 'WO, WO, WO!' You are attached to this universal sound and some crazy action. You've taken off your clothes just for this interview, but you don't understand true naked freedom yet. Sit down and I will tell you a story."

The man sat down, his face reddening. All of his confidence disappeared.

"There once was a man in southern China many, many years ago who never wore any clothes. In southern China, that was possible, because it is usually very hot. He wanted to be a completely free man, 100 percent completely free. So he never wore any clothes, every day for years on end. He sat all day under a tree. Sometimes he would go out begging for food, then go back to his tree to eat. Many people thought he was just crazy, but some people said, 'Waah, that's a completely free man!' So nobody could decide: is this man crazy, or completely free from life and death?

"Then one day, hearing of this man, the famous Zen Master Lin Chi said to one of his students, 'Make some beautiful clothes and take them to this naked ascetic. Perhaps he will have something interesting to say to you.' So the monk made the beautiful clothes and went to see him.

" 'How are you?' the student asked, coming upon the man fanning himself under a broad tree.

" 'Fine.'

" 'My teacher sent me over with these beautiful clothes.'

" 'That's not necessary!' the naked man said, waving off the monk. 'I already have some. And my clothes will never rip! The ones you have may be beautiful now, but in a few months? They'll be filthy and torn. The ones I have my parents gave me. They may get a little dirty from time to time, but then I just go swim in the river. And this one set has lasted my entire life! Two sets of clothing aren't necessary. Even you monks are less free than you realize, because you must always worry about robes and repairing clothing. But not me. I am free! So, please, take this unnecessary clothing back to your teacher.'

"This seemed to make sense to the Zen monk, and even impressive: the naked man's mind was not moving at all, and he seemed very happy and, well, so *free*! So the monk bowed politely and returned to his teacher, reporting everything the naked ascetic had said.

"Lin Chi told his student, 'Return to him tomorrow, and ask him this question: "Your parents gave you these natural clothes, but what kind of clothes did you have *before* your parents were born?" Then tell me what he says.' So the next day, the young monk again visited the naked man under his tree, and asked him Lin Chi's question.

"The naked man was completely stuck, and could not answer. He just sat there, scratching his head, scratching his seat. 'Before my parents were born, what kind of clothing? Before my parents were born, what kind of clothing?' His mind was completely stuck. It became a really big question for him; he stopped his daily begging, and stopped eating and bathing regularly. A few years passed, and the natural clothes his parents gave him began to wear out, and soon the naked ascetic died. He lost all the clothes his parents had given him. He was *completely* naked now!

"Many people came to his cremation. Afterward, as they sifted through his ashes, they discovered many *sarira*. These are crystallized remnants found in the cremated remains of especially great meditators. It is like ocean water that has been boiled off, leaving only salt. In Asia, when a great monk is cremated, many people will sift through the ashes to determine how many *sarira* remain. If none are produced, it means that the monk's virtue and practice were weak. But when *sarira* are produced—especially if there are a great number, or if they are especially novel in appearance—it is taken to mean that the monk has achieved extraordinary spiritual attainment or virtue in his life. This is an old Asian tradition for checking a monk's practice.

"So when the people saw these *sarira*, they said, 'Ahhh! This was a great monk! Too bad we never questioned him while he was still alive. All those years he spent walking around the streets naked, and we only noticed his rear end!'

"That night, Zen Master Lin Chi gave a Dharma talk in the temple. '*Sarira* might have a certain significance to some people,' he said. 'But the Buddha taught that form is emptiness; emptiness is form. So though you can see the *sarira*'s outside form, you must check them first to see if they are authentic!' Then he pointed his Zen stick at the *sarira*, which immediately turned to steam and disappeared right before everyone's eyes. Everybody was quite astonished! Then Lin Chi continued, 'This means, no form and no emptiness.' He pointed his stick again at the box where the *sarira* had been, and they suddenly reappeared! Lin Chi then said, 'Form is form; emptiness is emptiness.'

"The monks and laypeople gathered in the Dharma hall were totally dumbfounded. 'The Zen master's a magician!' they thought. 'How is this possible? We don't understand what's happening! Zen master, please explain.'

"At this, Lin Chi suddenly shouted, 'Hah! Are there any *sarira* now?!' Nobody could answer. The people were more confused than before, looking blankly at the Zen master, then at each other, then back at the Zen master.

"Seeing their consternation, Lin Chi continued, 'If any of you would understand the true meaning of my shout, that would be better for your life than finding one hundred pounds of holy *sarira*. Why are you all attached to these relics and remains? Why do you make "purity" and "impurity," "holy" and "unholy," "life" and "death"? This naked man was very pure, and when he died his cremated body produced many beautiful *sarira*. That is true. But he didn't understand his true self. That is very, very sad. Which is more important in Buddhism: producing crystallized jewels after death, or understanding your true self? If you understand your true self, that's better than one hundred pounds of *sarira*.' "

Concluding the story, Zen Master Seung Sahn looked at his naked student and asked, "So, before you were born, what kind of clothes did you have?"

The student stood up and said again, "WO, WO, WO!!"

Seung Sahn Sunim hit him with his Zen stick. BAM!

"*Ouch!*" the student screamed out.

"You are attached to your crazy action; you only understand 'WO, WO, WO!' That is not *your* true speech anymore, only some idea. But this 'Ouch!' is from your original body. It comes from your just-now body. 'Ouch!' is just-like-this. But only saying 'WO, WO, WO!' means you are attached to emptiness, to the realm of no name and no form. If you're attached just to saying 'WO, WO, WO!' then you don't understand the true meaning of 'WO, WO, WO!' so you better put your clothes back on."

"Oh, yes, OK. Thank you very much." Meekly covering his private parts, the student bowed and left.

Good Things

A STUDENT ONCE ASKED Zen Master Seung Sahn's grand-teacher, the legendary Zen Master Man Gong, "Why don't more people practice Zen meditation?"

"People live their whole lives with the hope that good things will always come to them. But they don't know that when you get a good thing, you also get a bad thing. That is just the rule of this universe. Then they are surprised at getting this bad thing, and suffer. For all their lives, they go around and around and around, chasing good things, avoiding what is unpleasant.

"So, as you practice the Way, you have to give up this human route. You must become deaf, dumb, and blind, and refrain from chasing and avoiding things. Don't make anything. Don't want anything. Then your true self will be realized naturally."

Natural Style

POEM BY ZEN MASTER Man Gong

Even Buddha and eminent teachers are not my friends.
How do you become friends with the blue ocean?
I am originally Korean,
So, naturally I stand like this, of course.

Tollbooth Bodhisattva

ONE AFTERNOON, Zen Master Seung Sahn and several of his students were driving down Route I-95, from Providence, Rhode Island, to New York City. They chatted from time to time as they drove, with the students asking him questions about various things. At one point they stopped at a tollbooth. The driver handed the tollbooth operator some money, and was waiting for his change. One of the students said to her through the open window, "Nice day, isn't it?"

"Yes," she replied. "But, my goodness, where did all this wind come from?" After she gave them their change, the car drove off.

The car was quiet for several miles. Then Zen Master Seung Sahn turned to his students and said, "That was no ordinary woman at the tollbooth. That was Kwan Seum Bosal [the Bodhisattva of compassion] asking you a great question: 'Where did all this wind come from?' What a wonderful *kong-an*! You must always be alert to the teaching that comes your way, all the time. Let go of your mind and then you can see what's actually in front of you. So I ask you, where did all this wind come from?"

No one could answer.

"OK. I'll give you a hint. Zen Master Man Gong wrote a poem that will help you:

Everything is born by following the wind;
everything dies by following the wind.
When you find out where the wind comes from,
there is no life, no death.

When you have an answer 'like-this,'
You see nature through spiritual eyes."

Poison Arrow

ZEN MASTER SEUNG SAHN said to an assembly of students, "Many people think that intellectual understanding can help them, and help this world. But that is not possible: intellectual understanding is only someone else's *idea* about something. Whatever you read in books and hear in lectures, that's not *your* thing. If you understand things only intellectually, then you will not understand this world, as it is. Then you will suffer, and make suffering for others.

"You've heard about how the Native Americans dipped arrowheads into poison, and then shot them at something? Having too much intellectual understanding is like being hit with one of these poison arrows. You have to pull it out quickly, correct? But most people who have this arrow stuck in them only *think* about the arrow, instead of pulling it out: 'Where did this arrow come from?' 'Who shot it?' 'How was it shot?' 'How was it made?' 'Is this arrow like other poison arrows?' 'What kind of wood is this?' 'How tall was the shooter?' 'Was his nose long, or flat?' Lots of thinking, thinking, thinking, thinking, thinking.

"But soon the body will die! This thinking and analyzing are not necessary—first pull out the arrow, and then the poison cannot spread any further. But many people won't take out the arrow of suffering that is in their minds; they only spend time and money and energy analyzing and thinking and reading about it! 'Where did this arrow come from?' 'Who made it, and who shot it?' 'Where was it shot from?' 'Why was it shot?' 'How does an arrow move through the air?' 'How fast did it travel here?'

"That kind of mind is like most human beings: 'Why is there suffering?' 'Where does suffering come from?' 'Why is this world so complicated?' 'What does So-and-so write about it?' All this checking, checking, checking, checking, and not one bit of 'What am *I*?' They do not look into their not-knowing mind. People don't realize that this don't-know mind already cuts off all thinking, already pulls out the arrow. If you first take out the arrow, then a thinking mind is no problem. But if you don't take it out, then any kind of thinking and checking mind that appears will kill you. And everybody dies, because everyone is checking their minds like this. Only very few people actually try to take out this arrow, so you who do meditation are all very special, very lucky. Your '*What am I?*' cuts through this poison."

Special-Practice Monks

In South Korea there is a famous mountain called Ji Ri Sahn Mountain, and on this mountain there is an ancient Zen temple, called Chon Un Sah Temple. It has been there for many hundreds of years, and was built even before Zen was a great movement in Korea. For centuries, the temple was supported by the devoted lay Buddhist people in the area, and also by the region's governor, who was a devout Buddhist himself.

One year, a new governor was appointed to that region. He was a Confucian, so he didn't like Buddhism at all. Buddhism had been a national religion in Korea for many centuries when Confucians took power during the Chosun Dynasty (1492–1910), and Buddhism was often repressed by different kings and local officials. Buddhist monks in particular had a very difficult situation.

So in those times it was quite usual for the new governor to make trouble for the people who had anything to do with the temples in his district. One day, he summoned the temple's abbot. When the monk arrived at the regional office, the governor didn't say a word, and simply hit him on the top of his head very hard. "Why did you hit me?" the abbot asked.

"You're very bad," the governor replied. "Your students don't do any work. They only sit in that meditation room all day, doing nothing for hours on end. I see all these hardworking people give them food, and the monks only eat, lie down, and sleep. I don't like that! They're all a bunch of rice thieves! Everyone in this world has to work, but not these monks of yours. So now you must pay higher taxes to the government." Then he hit the abbot a few more times.

"OK, we will of course pay these new taxes," the abbot said, even though his temple was small and very poor, and had never had to pay taxes before. He left the governor's office and went back to the temple. When he arrived, the kitchen master saw the abbot's face. He saw that he was very sad.

"What happened with the governor?" he asked, and the abbot told him everything that had befallen him at the governor's office. When the abbot had finished, the monks fell into a long silence together.

After a few minutes, the kitchen master's face suddenly brightened up. "Waah, I have a good idea! We'll invite the governor over. Tell him how poor we are, and that we have no money—but tell him that we have all of these valuable antiques and ancient works of art. Tell him that if he likes any, he can take one." The kitchen master knew that the governor was very, very corrupt, and that these things were better than money for him.

"That's a wonderful plan. But there is only one problem," the abbot said. "We don't *have* any antiques. We don't have any priceless works of art. How are we supposed to give him such things if we don't even have them ourselves? Are you crazy?" He looked very confused.

"Don't worry, don't worry," the kitchen master said. "You just get him to come over. I'll take care of the rest."

"OK," the abbot said, squinting narrowly at his crafty kitchen master. He had known this young monk since he had entered the temple. The kitchen master practiced meditation very hard, so maybe he had some special plan . . .

The kitchen master prepared lots of good food and drink. He sent several monks to the garden to collect the freshest vegetables. Special rice cakes were rolled out, sliced, and dusted with pine-nut powder. They baked and fried the most delicious temple delicacies, things eaten only on special days, like Buddha's Birthday. Everyone was very excited! They were also very curious about the kitchen master's plan.

After a short while, the abbot returned, with the governor right behind him. The governor rubbed his hands, and his eyes glanced nervously from side to side. The monks put all of the delicious food out for him, and invited him to eat.

But the governor did not seem to be interested in food at all. He was only interested in seeing where the beautiful antiques were, and what he could choose for himself. As the monks tried to make him comfortable, he grew impatient. "Abbot, I want to see those antiques! Where are they?"

The abbot called out, "Kitchen Master!"

"Yes, sir?"

"It's time to bring out the antiques!"

"Yes, sir! Coming right out!" the kitchen master yelled back, and went into the kitchen for a minute. All that was heard was the sound of various objects being tossed hither and thither, an empty jar falling down, a glass bottle breaking. Everybody was very nervous!

When he finally came out, he was carrying only a broom!

Bowing deeply at the waist, with a grand gesture he offered it up to the governor.

The governor got *very* angry. "You stupid monk! Who do you think I am? That's just a broom! That can't be more than a month old!"

The kitchen master looked genuinely surprised. "But that's not true, Your Excellency! This is a very valuable and powerful treasure."

The governor exploded into rage. "Do you take me for a fool? I am governor of this whole area! Who do you think you're talking to?"

All the other monks trembled in fear, because this man was very, very powerful. But the kitchen master wasn't afraid at all. With his eyes closed and chin out slightly, he had a broad, confident smile on his face. "This broom is very, very old. It was made many thousands of years ago. If you ride this broom even once, you can fly through the sky!"

"Fly?" The governor looked at him. "Is that *true*?"

"Yes, Your Excellency. That's *true*!"

"OK," the governor said. "Then you try it first."

"No problem, I'll go first. But you must not think anything about what you see. Don't think good and bad. Only keep a clear mind!"

"OK," the governor replied.

So the kitchen master put the broom between his legs and—*ppssheewww!!*—flew off into the sky! He circled the temple once and landed in front of the governor. The governor couldn't believe his eyes—the monk had really flown through the air! The governor rubbed his hands together and said, "Ahhhh, I must have this broom!"

But the kitchen master only looked at him, "Your Excellency!"

"Yes?" he replied, very afraid now of this monk.

"It's your turn. Try it once."

"Is it possible?"

"If your mind is good, then riding this broom is possible. If your mind is bad, then it will be impossible to move even one inch."

"But my mind is not bad!" the governor said.

"We know that, we know that," the kitchen master said, smiling. "But this broom understands your mind. So try for yourself."

The governor put the broom between his legs, squeezed his eyes tight, and jumped. And jumped. And jumped. But he didn't go anywhere!

"You're no good, Your Excellency," the kitchen master said. "You're always doing many bad actions, so you cannot fly anywhere on the broom. Everybody else can fly except for you. I am only the kitchen master at this temple, and even I can fly it. The abbot flies on it all the time." The governor was speechless, completely stuck.

Then the kitchen master pointed in the direction of the main meditation hall. "There are many monks over there, and they have special energy. They can just point at you, and—boom!—they can give you an electric shock! All they do all day is meditate. Anytime you do some bad action, no matter how small, they can perceive it. Sometimes they wake up if they sense you doing something wrong, and they can send electricity over to shock you. So you must keep a clear mind. Do you want to see inside the meditation hall?"

"Yes, sir. Yes, sir," the governor said.

"Then come on over. We can't open the door. But just wet your finger and push it through the rice-paper window, like this, and look inside." When they peered into the room, they saw the monks sitting in many different positions. Some sat slumped forward, their chins resting against their chests; some sat with their heads tilted way back and to the side; while another sat slumped over to the left. They sat all different kinds of ways.

The governor asked, "Those people sitting slumped forward—what kind of meditation is this?"

"That's perceive-the-ground meditation," the kitchen master replied.

"And what kind of meditation is this, the ones with their heads falling backward with their mouths wide open?"

"That's perceive-the-ceiling meditation."

"And that guy slumped over to the left?"

"That's dancing meditation."

"Oh," the governor said, "How wonderful! There really are many kinds of meditation!"

"Of course!" the kitchen master replied. "These great monks use any kind of meditation only to help this world. When they finish one kind of meditation, they go on to another kind. My style is only broom-riding meditation. I don't use anything to do this: the body disappears and becomes smoke, and can come and go anywhere with no hindrance. When you return home, if you do some bad action, these meditation monks' bodies can also change, become smoke, and go into your room and kill you."

"OK! OK!" the governor shouted. "No taxes for this temple! Before, I didn't understand these people, but now I'll only support you! I'll do anything I can; anything at all." So the governor left and went back to his palace. He never bothered the meditating monks of Chon Un Sah Temple ever again.

Beginning of This World

SOMEONE ASKED Zen Master Seung Sahn, "What do you think about the beginning of this world?

"The beginning of this world came from your mouth. Ha ha ha! Do you understand?"

The student was silent.

"Then I will explain: what is this world? You must understand that point first. You make time, space, cause and effect. In three seconds, when you asked that question, you made this whole world. Science used to teach that time and space, and cause and effect, are absolutes. But modern physics teaches that time, space, and cause and effect are subjective. So you make this whole world, and you make your time and space."

The student said, "I still don't understand."

Dae Soen Sa Nim replied, "OK, so first you must understand, what is time? One unit of time is an hour. But my thinking sometimes makes this hour very long, or very short. You go to the airport to pick up your girlfriend. You haven't seen her in a long time. You wait at the airport, and the airplane is very late. Five, ten, twenty, thirty minutes—waiting, waiting, waiting. Even another hour passes. Ten minutes seems like a whole day. And this one hour passes like an eternity because you want to see her very much, and you sit there saying, 'Where is the plane? Why hasn't it arrived yet?' But yet some other time, you go dancing with friends, and dance all night, and even one hour seems to pass by very quickly. Now that same amount of time measured as 'one hour' seems very short. 'A *whole* hour has already passed? It seems like only a minute!' So mind makes one hour very long or very short. Time depends on thinking, because time is created by thinking. The Buddha taught this, and we can test it in our everyday life: 'Everything is created by mind alone.'

"It is the same with space: Spain is here, and New York is there, Korea is over there, and Japan is over here. People in Spain say, 'This way is north, that's south, east, and west.' But on the opposite side of the earth, Korean people say that north is here, south is over there, and east and west are here and here. If I stay here, my north, south, east, and west are like this. If I am not here, my north, south, east, and west disappear. Cause and effect are also the same: if I do some good action, I go to heaven; bad action, go to hell. That's cause and effect. But if I don't make anything, where do I go?

"So I make time, and space, and cause and effect. I make my world; you make your world. A cat makes a cat's world. A dog makes a dog's world. God makes God's world. Buddha makes Buddha's world. If you believe in God 100 percent, then when you die, and your world disappears, you go to God's world. If you believe in Buddha 100 percent, then when your world disappears, you will go to Buddha's world. But if you believe in your true self 100 percent, then you make your world, and that's complete freedom: heaven or hell, coming and going anywhere with no hindrance."

Dae Soen Sa Nim looked at the questioner. "So I ask you, which one do you like?"

The student was silent.

"Anytime you open your mouth, your world appears."

The student asked, "So, who was the first person to open his mouth?"

"You already understand!"

Amid general laughter, the student was silent for a few moments. Then he bowed deeply.

Why Are We Here?

SOMEONE ASKED Zen Master Seung Sahn, "Why are we here?"

"Why did you come here today?"

"Because I wanted to come."

"What do you want?"

"Well, I want happiness," the student replied.

"Correct! But, where do you come from? What is your name?"

"Juan."

"That's only your *body's* name. What is your true self's name?"

The student was puzzled for a moment, and then said, "Somebody gave me this name, Juan. That's my only name."

"Yes, that is your body's name: that's not *your* name. Somebody gave you that name. Before that, you had no name. So this name is not you. You may say, 'This is my hand, that's my head, this is my body.' But it's not you. Your body has a master. Please bring your master here."

The student was silent.

"Who is your master?"

The student replied, "I don't know."

"You don't know. That's your true name. Someone might call it mind, or soul, or consciousness, while someone else calls it nature. But your true name, what is it really called?" The student was still silent. "OK, how old are you?"

"I'm thirty years old," the student replied.

"That's your *body's* age. That's not your true age. Another question: when you die, where will you go?"

"I don't know."

"Correct! You don't understand your coming into this world, or your leaving. You don't know your name or age, or any kind of coming or going. So you are 'don't know.' That's your true self. A long time ago, Socrates used to walk through the streets of Athens, telling everyone he saw, 'You must understand your true self! You must understand your true self!' One day, a student asked him, "Teacher, do *you* understand *your* true self?' Socrates replied, 'I don't know. But I understand this don't-know, this not-knowing.' That's a very important point. If you attain your don't-know, then you understand your true self. This don't-know mind is very important."

"Well," the student continued, "What is this don't-know?"

Dae Soen Sa Nim replied, "When you're thinking, your mind and my mind are different. When you cut off all thinking, your mind, my mind, and everybody's minds are the same: God's mind, Buddha's mind, Christ's mind, Kwan Seum Bosal's mind, demon's mind, any mind is the same mind. Then there is no Russian, no American, no Spanish or Korean. Your before-thinking mind already cuts off all thinking. Zen means cutting off all this thinking, and then world peace is no problem. In the past, Russians and Americans were always fighting each other's ideas. 'I like communism,' 'I like capitalism.' Zen means putting it all down, cutting off all thinking, and returning to your pure and clear original nature. Then you can perceive that your mind and my mind are actually the same mind.

"So, if you don't understand your mind, only go straight, *don't know*. Then your don't-know mind, my don't-know mind, and somebody else's don't-know mind are the same don't-know mind. This don't-know mind already stops thinking; when you stop thinking, there's no thinking. No thinking means empty mind; empty mind is *before* thinking. Your before-thinking is your substance. My before-thinking is my substance. (Holding out his Zen stick.) Then this stick's substance, universal substance, and everything's substance is the same substance.

"So when you keep this don't-know mind 100 percent, you are the universe and the universe is you. You and everything already become one. A name for that is *primary point*. Don't know is not 'don't know'; don't know is primary point. The *name* for primary point is *don't know*. Now, somebody may say that primary point is 'mind,' 'Buddha,' 'God,' 'nature,' 'substance,' 'the absolute,' 'universal energy,' 'holiness,' or 'consciousness.' But the true primary point has no name, no form, no speech, no words: it's before thinking, while these names are all *after* thinking—they are made by thinking. Opening your mouth is already a big mistake. But when you keep a don't-know mind 100 percent, you and everything already become one.

"So I ask you, keeping a don't-know mind, this stick, this sound (hitting the table), and you—are they the same or different?"

The student replied, "I don't really understand what you mean. I have a problem with . . ."

"Yes, you are thinking, so you don't understand. Your *thinking* is the problem. But my question is very simple. I already told you to keep a don't-know mind. That means cut off all thinking. At that time, this stick's substance, this sound's substance (hitting the table), and your substance—are they the same or different?"

The student replied, "The same."

"If you say 'the same,' I will hit you. If you say 'different,' I will also hit you. If you say you have a problem, I will also hit you. Ha ha ha ha! Because primary point is before thinking, there are no speech or words that can express it. Opening your mouth is already a big mistake. So, are they the same or different?"

The student said, "I don't know."

"OK, not bad. But one more step is necessary! Ha ha ha ha! You keep this don't-know mind, anytime and anyplace. Then soon some answer will appear. If you want to check your answer, go ask a tree. This tree's answer will help you very much. Also, the barking of a dog is a very good teacher, better than Zen masters. But first you must keep a don't-know mind. That is very important, OK?"

The student bowed. "Thank you very much."

The Sixth Patriarch's Mistake

SEVERAL YEARS AGO, Zen Master Seung Sahn and several of his students visited China, in search of the temples and sites most associated with the history of Zen in that country. They met many Chinese Buddhist monks and Zen teachers, and were greeted warmly wherever they went.

The first site they visited was Liu Rong Temple, in Guangzhou, a 1,450-year-old Rinzai temple. Zen Master Seung Sahn and his students were taken on a tour through the temple by the abbot, Master Sul Bong, who pointed out the various structures and some of the restoration projects undertaken to repair damage inflicted during the Cultural Revolution. Eventually, they reached the Hall of the Sixth Patriarch. Everyone was very honored to be there, and very impressed.

They toured the interior of the hall, on the wall of which was written the Sixth Patriarch's famous poem. To students of the Zen school, this poem has great importance for the founding of the tradition in China. But for Chinese monks especially, this poem is considered with almost a sacred reverence, for it contains within its compact frame the absolute essence of Patriarchal Zen.

This is the story of the poem: Many years ago, the Fifth Patriarch had offered to give Dharma Transmission to anyone who could express the essence of mind in four lines of verse. The head monk at the temple, Shin Hsiu, responded with the following verse:

> Our body is the Bodhi tree.
> Mind is clear mirror's stand.
> Diligently polishing it,
> No dust remains.

Layman No heard about this poem, and immediately expressed his view of the essence of mind as follows:

> Bodhi has no tree;
> Clear mirror has no stand.
> Originally nothing;
> Where could dust remain?

When the Fifth Patriarch read Layman No's poem, he thought it far superior to the head monk's poem, and gave Dharma Transmission to Layman No. Layman No thus became the Sixth Patriarch.

As the abbot of Liu Rong Temple, Zen Master Seung Sahn, and his students looked at the poem on the wall in the Hall of the Sixth Patriarch, Dae Soen Sa Nim said, "With this poem, Hui Neng was recognized and became the Sixth Patriarch. But there's a mistake in this poem. You are the abbot of this temple; do you see the Sixth Patriarch's mistake?"

Visibly shocked, the abbot gestured at the poem. "A mistake? The Sixth Patriarch? I could not imagine. . . . On which line?"

"No, no," Seung Sahn Sunim replied. "Not these lines—the lines are all correct. The *characters* are all correct. But the meaning is a big mistake. If you say, 'Originally nothing,' that's already a big mistake. Because if you truly believe there's originally nothing, you cannot even *write* or *say* 'originally nothing.' The Sixth Patriarch said, 'Originally nothing,' which means that there is something that says 'Originally nothing.' That *makes* something. That is the first mistake.

"Also, the Sixth Patriarch has made three dusts—'originally nothing' dust, 'Bodhi' dust, and 'clear mirror has no stand' dust. So how can he say, in the last line, 'Where could dust remain?' There are already many, many dusts in this poem. That's a contradiction! So this whole poem is a big mistake." Then, looking at the abbot, whose eyes remained widened from shock, Dae Soen Sa Nim asked, "How would you correct this poem?"

The abbot replied, "Well, when the Sixth Patriarch wrote 'Originally nothing,' he was referring to the phrase in the *Diamond Sutra*: 'All formations are impermanent; if you view all appearance as nonappearance, you can see true nature.' That's what the Sixth Patriarch meant."

Dae Soen Sa Nim said, "Yes, that is the principle of emptiness. The head monk wrote about 'form is emptiness, emptiness is form.' The Sixth Patriarch's poem shows 'no form, no emptiness.' In other words, the head monk is attached to the impermanence of the phenomenal world, whereas the Sixth Patriarch is attached to emptiness. That all makes sense—intellectually. But the true world is 'form is form, emptiness is emptiness.' Would you please hit the Sixth Patriarch's poem from the point of view of 'form is form, emptiness is emptiness'?"

The abbot said, "Oh, in that reality, opening the mouth is already a mistake."

"Then how can you open your mouth even to say that?"

The abbot covered his mouth with his hands and said, "Oh, yes, I made a mistake."

Where Is the Real Buddha?

WHILE TRAVELING IN CHINA, Zen Master Seung Sahn and several of his students visited the Fa Yuan Temple, in Beijing. They were taken on a tour around the temple by the house master, after which they were joined by the resident master, Chuan Yin, for tea and light cakes. After exchanging pleasantries for a few minutes, Dae Soen Sa Nim said to Chuan Yin, "This temple is very wonderful. There are many, many Buddha statues in this temple—big buddhas, little buddhas. Tell me, which one is the real Buddha?"

Chuan Yin answered by writing, "Where there is no Buddha, you should pass through rapidly; where there is a Buddha, you should not stop and stay." This is a line from a classic old *kong-an*.

Dae Soen Sa Nim replied, "That's only an explanation. I don't like explanations. Please tell me where the true Buddha is."

Chuan Yin hesitated for a few moments.

Then Dae Soen Sa Nim said, "The true Buddha is sitting on the chair, is he not?"

"Me?" the abbot said, very surprised. Then he and Dae Soen Sa Nim held hands and laughed.

God's Substance

A WOMAN ONCE ASKED Zen Master Seung Sahn, "Do you believe in God?"

"Of course!"

She became perplexed. "You are a Buddhist monk, and a Zen master, at that. How can you possibly believe in God?"

"I can believe my hands. I believe in my eyes, ears, nose, tongue, body, and mind. Why not believe in God? If you believe in your true self completely, then you can believe that the sky is blue, the tree is green, the dog is barking 'Woof! Woof!' It's very simple, yah?"

The woman was silent for a moment.

Zen Master Seung Sahn continued, "Buddhism teaches, 'One by one, each thing is complete.' That means that your mind is complete. How is your mind complete? (Hits the floor with his Zen stick.) Just this point. Did you hear that? (Hits the floor.) That point is already complete. If you're thinking, it's not complete. But in this moment (hits the floor), just hear that sound. At that moment, this sound and you (hits the floor) already become one, which means you and the universe already become one. This means there's no subject, no object;

no inside, no outside. Inside and outside already become one. The name for that is *absolute,* or *truth.*

"So if you keep this mind (hits the floor), your mind is already complete. The sun, the moon, the stars, and everything are already complete. Your sound and my sound are the same. This sound (hits the floor) is your substance: this sound's substance and your substance already become one; my substance and this sound's substance already become one. It's the same substance as the sun, the moon, and the stars—any substance is the same substance. So Buddhism teaches, 'Each thing has it. It and dust interpenetrate.' This means that sound's substance, and name and form, already become one. Let us consider ice, water, and steam. The names and forms are different, but fundamentally it is all still H_2O. Water is H_2O. Ice is H_2O. Steam is also H_2O. Name and form are different, and constantly change according to conditions, but the substance is the same."

"But this seems so difficult, and not related at all to the question of God," the woman said.

"Put it all down, OK? If you're thinking, this seems very difficult. If you're not thinking, it's no problem. If you're thinking, you make 'I,' 'my,' and 'me.' Descartes said, 'I think, therefore I am.' Thinking makes *I*; thinking makes everything. But if you are not thinking, then what? When you are thinking, you make this whole universe, you make everything. And then 'I' and 'God' and 'Buddha' and everything are separate. But if you keep this point (hits the floor)—*this* moment—then you and God are never separate. It's very easy, yah?"

Dog Kills Joju

ZEN MASTER SEUNG SAHN and several others were once invited to stay at a student's house out in the country. The student had a large dog, which spent most of the time looking out the front door, wagging its tail and barking anytime someone came near the house. In the evening, as everyone was resting around the fireplace after dinner, the dog came and sat next to Dae Soen Sa Nim.

The Zen master leaned over to the dog. "I have a question for you that all Zen students cannot answer: Buddha said that all things have Buddha-nature. But when asked if a dog has Buddha-nature, the great Zen Master Joju said, '*Mu!*' ('No!') So I ask you, do you have Buddha-nature?"

"Woof! Woof! Woof!"

"You are better than Joju," Dae Soen Sa Nim said.

Understanding Nothing, Attaining Nothing

A STUDENT ONCE ASKED Zen Master Seung Sahn, "How do we attain emptiness? Sometimes I have a feeling of emptiness, like everything is meaningless. But I suspect that this is not the kind of emptiness that the Buddha wanted us to find. Or am I wrong?"

Zen Master Seung Sahn replied, "The kind of empty feeling that you are talking about is not true emptiness. It is a kind of feeling-emptiness. It is based on attachment to feelings and conditions. As soon as those feelings or conditions change, the emptiness disappears, yah?"

"Yes, that's right," the student replied.

"Then that's not true emptiness. True emptiness is insight into the nature of the universe, and is never changing. But many people only follow their attachments, so when they are disappointed, everything feels meaningless, and empty.

"I like to explain it this way: Recently I had a visit from a very strong student of mine, Mr. Ku. He is seventy years old, and came to the U.S. from Korea to visit his daughter. We all drove to Plymouth Rock together, because Mr. Ku wanted to see where America began. Then we all had supper and went to sit by the ocean. I asked him, 'You are a Buddhist, a wonderful student. What have you gotten from this life?'

" 'Nothing,' he said.

"Mr. Ku is the president of a very successful business in Korea. He lives in the most beautiful home in Seoul. Some of his children are living in the U.S., and some in Korea. His brother owns a famous food company. He and his family and all his children are all very rich, very high class. So I said to him, 'Your daughter has a nice house; she is very happy.'

"He said, 'I don't know. Very nice house? Happy? What kind of happiness? I don't know.' Then he said, 'What is correct happiness, anyway?'

"He already understands what correct happiness is. He is seventy years old, and has seen everything happen. In his life, he's had many good things. Many things have happened to him. Much has appeared and disappeared in his life. Up, down, up, down, up, down. Finally, he will soon die, but when I asked him, 'What did you attain?' he said, 'Nothing.'

"What kind of nothing is this? Understanding nothing is not the same thing as attaining nothing. If you only understand nothing, you still have a problem. If you understand nothing, then you see your life as being like a cloud, like lightning, like dew. 'Everything is changing, changing, changing. All form is always changing. So everything is nothing, and therefore my life is also nothing. Form is emptiness, so my life is empty, nothing.' If you only understand this, we say you are attached to emptiness, and you cannot function moment to moment for others. It is a kind of alienation, and in its extreme form, nihilism. This happens to many people.

"But if you *attain* nothing, then everything is no problem. Then your house is correct, your mind is correct, your action is correct, your nature is correct. That's because if you attain nothing, there is no form, no emptiness. But if you say, 'No form, no emptiness,' this is also thinking; and if you say 'Nothing,' you don't understand nothing. When you correctly attain nothing, there is no speech, no word. Then what? Form is form, emptiness is emptiness. Everything is just-like-this.

"So, if you were seventy years old, and someone asked you, 'What did you attain?' how would you answer?"

(A student hits the floor.)

"Not bad. But if you have no hands, then what? Ha ha ha ha! So I ask you: before you were born, you had no eyes, no ears, no nose, no tongue, no body, and no mind. Now you have eyes, ears, nose, tongue, body, and mind. Sometime soon, you will die, and again have no eyes, no ears, no nose, no tongue, no body, and no mind. The thing that you think is you is only a temporary condition: it has no true nature of its own. Then what? Then what are *you*? This is very important! If someone here answers by hitting the floor, this is not bad, not good. But if you have no body, how can you hit? *Hit* means understanding emptiness. But if you correctly *attain* emptiness, then what? Be careful!

"So, understanding emptiness, and feeling a kind of emptiness: none of these can help your life. But if you look very deeply inside—'*What am I?*'—then you can *attain* true emptiness, and help this whole world. Understand?"

The student bowed, "Thank you for your teaching."

Attaining Nothing, Part Two

A MONK RUSHED UP to Zen Master Seung Sahn at Hwa Gye Sah Temple in Seoul. "Zen Master, I have attained nothing-I! I am completely free!"

"You have attained nothing-I?"

"Yes, I have completely attained! There is no I! Ha ha ha ha!"

"So I ask you, Who has attained nothing-I?"

The monk said, "I have attained nothing-I."

Dae Soen Sa Nim hit him.

"Ouch!"

Dae Soen Sa Nim said, "If you have completely attained nothing, who said 'Ouch?'"

The monk was completely stuck, and could not answer.

"If you completely attain nothing-I, how can you say 'I'? How can you say 'freedom'? How can you even open your mouth?"

The monk hesitated for a few moments. "But I . . . I . . ." Then, realizing his mistake, he bowed deeply to Dae Soen Sa Nim.

"You must find this mouth's true master. Don't make 'I,' don't make 'freedom,' don't make 'nothing,' don't make *anything*."

Zen Math

THE FOLLOWING EXCHANGE took place between Zen Master Seung Sahn and a questioner at the Dharma Zen Center in Los Angeles:

Questioner: What is Zen?

Dae Soen Sa Nim: What are you?

Q: (Silence.)

DSSN: Do you understand?

Q: I don't know.

DSSN: This don't-know mind is you. Zen is understanding yourself, "What am I?"

Q: Is that all there is to Zen?

DSSN: Isn't it enough?

Q: I mean, there must be a final understanding or illumination that a Zen master has in order to be a Zen master.

DSSN: All understanding is no understanding. What do *you* understand? Show me!

Q: (Silence.)

DSSN: OK, what is one plus two?

Q: Three.

DSSN: Correct! Why didn't you tell me *that*? (Laughter from the assembly.) What color is the sky?

Q: Blue.

DSSN: Very good! (Laughter.) The truth is very simple, yah? But your mind is too complicated; you understand too much. So at first you could not answer. But you don't understand one thing.

Q: What?

DSSN: One plus two equals zero.

Q: I don't see how that could be.

DSSN: OK. Suppose someone gives me an apple. I eat it. Then he gives me two more apples. I eat them. All the apples are gone. So, one plus two equals zero.

Q: Hmmm . . .

DSSN: You must understand this. Before you were born, you were zero. Now, you are one. Very soon, you will die and again become zero. All things in the universe are like this. They arise from emptiness and return to emptiness. So zero equals one; one equals zero.

Q: I see that.

DSSN: In elementary school, they teach you that one plus two equals three. In our Zen elementary school, we lead sentient beings to the insight that one plus two equals zero. Which one is correct?

Q: Both.

DSSN: If you say "both," I say "neither."

Q: Why?

DSSN: If you say they are both true, then rockets cannot possibly go to the moon. (Laughter.) When one plus two only equals three, then a rocket can reach the moon. But if one plus two *also* equals zero, then on the way up, the spaceship will disappear. Then this astronaut has a problem! Ha ha ha ha! (Extended laughter from the assembly.) So I say, neither is correct.

Q: Then what would be a proper answer?

DSSN: "Both" is a wrong answer, so I hit you. Also, "neither" is wrong, so I hit myself. (Laughter.) The first teaching in Buddhism is "Form is emptiness; emptiness is form." This means that one equals zero; zero equals one. But who makes form? Who makes emptiness? Both form and emptiness are concepts, ideas. Concepts are made by your own thinking. Descartes said, "I think, therefore I am." But if I am not thinking, then what? Before thinking, there is no you or I, no form or emptiness, no right or wrong, no one or two or three. So even saying "No form, no emptiness" is wrong. In true emptiness, before thinking, you only keep a clear mind. All things are just as they are: form is form, emptiness is emptiness.

Q: I'm afraid I still don't understand.

DSSN: If you want to understand, that's already a big mistake. Just keep the question *"What am I?"* Only go straight and keep a don't-know mind 100 percent. Then you will understand everything. Then this whole universe will become yours, OK?

Q: Thank you.

I Want to Die!

ONE DAY, a man came into Hwa Gye Sah Temple outside Seoul. He was very anxious, and shouting, "I want to die! I want to die! I want to die!"

A monk approached him and asked, "What's wrong?"

"I want to die!"

"Just a moment," the monk said. "What's wrong? Why do you want to die?"

"I don't like this world! I don't like people! I don't like anything! I only want to DIE!!"

"OK, you dying is no problem," the monk said. "But we have this famous Zen master here. So you should first talk to him. Maybe he can help you understand your mind before you die."

The man agreed, and the next day he was introduced to Zen Master Seung Sahn. "I want to die, Zen master. I don't like this world anymore. It is only a sea of suffering. So I want to die."

"You're already dead," Dae Soen Sa Nim said.

"I'm dead?" the man shouted. "What do you mean? I'm not dead yet!"

"You're already dead."

"I'm not dead!"

"When you say 'I'm not dead,' only your mouth is still alive. But you're already dead."

"What does that mean?"

"Already dead," Dae Soen Sa Nim continued. "Who are you? Why are you dragging this corpse around?"

"I'm not dragging any corpse around."

"Why are you dragging this corpse around? What is a human being? Show me! If you want to die, then *die*. But before that, what are *you*? You say 'I want to die.' Who wants to die? What is this 'I'? Who?"

The man was completely stuck, and could not say anything.

"So, you're already dead. Now you must wake up!"

"OK, Zen master."

"If you really want to die, killing your body is not the way. That's not real dying, only 'body-dying.' So if you really want to die, then with all of your energy you must only keep this question: '*What am I? What am I? What am I?*' You say, 'I want to die.' This 'I' comes from where? What are *you*?"

"Don't know."

"Don't know! Correct! So you must deeply perceive this don't-know mind. If you completely attain this don't-know, there is no life and no death. Then living is no problem; dying is also no problem. OK?"

"There is no life and death?" The student bowed deeply. "Thank you for your teaching."

Making Life and Death

AFTER A DHARMA TALK at the New Haven Zen Center, a student asked Zen Master Seung Sahn, "Does one have to go through the pain of life and death in order to experience empty mind?"

Dae Soen Sa Nim said, "I ask you, where are you coming from—from life or from death?"

"From life, of course," the student replied.

Dae Soen Sa Nim asked, "From life? What is life?"

The student could not answer for a few moments, then said, "Ego."

"Ego? What is ego?"

The student did not answer.

Dae Soen Sa Nim lifted his cup. "This is water, right? Now its temperature is maybe 65 degrees. If you lower the temperature to 20 degrees, the water becomes ice. If you raise it past 212 degrees, it becomes steam. You see water, but as the temperature changes, its form appears and disappears, appears and disappears. Water to ice to steam to water again. That is the form changing. The substance of H_2O does not appear and disappear, only the form changes. Water, ice, and steam are only names and forms. Names and forms are always changing, but H_2O does not change. If you understand the temperature, you can understand the form.

"So you ask about death. What is your true self? These are your hands, your legs, and your body. Your body has life and death. But your true self has no life, no death. You think, 'My body is me. This is what I am.' But this is not correct. It is just a form, not truly 'you.' So to think 'I' or 'passing through death'—this is crazy; you must wake up!

"Water, ice, and steam are all H_2O, but if you are attached to water and then the water becomes ice, then you will say the water disappears. So it must be 'dead!' But raise the temperature, and—*boom!*—the water is 'born' again! If you keep raising the temperature, the water will disappear and become steam. So the water must be 'dead' again!

Don't be attached to 'water.' This is only name and form. Name and form are originally empty; they're always changing, changing, changing, changing. Name and form are made by thinking. Water never says, 'I am water.' The sun never says, 'I am the sun.' The moon never says, 'I am the moon.' Human beings say 'water.' Human beings say 'sun' and 'moon.' So you see, name and form are empty—they have no self-nature. They only come from thinking. Life and death are also like that.

"If you are attached to name and form, you cannot understand H_2O, and you cannot correctly use water, ice, and steam. Attachment to name and form means attachment to outside appearances. The *Diamond Sutra* says, 'If you view all appearance as nonappearance, this view is Buddha.' That's the same point.

"So first you must cut off all thinking, and then your mind

will become completely empty. Then you can perceive truth, which is just-like-this. That is finding the correct function of water, the correct function of ice, the correct function of steam. The truth is just-like-this, very easy. Then your true self can function correctly to help all beings, from moment to moment. And that is the correct function of life and death."

The student bowed deeply and said, "Thank you for your teaching."

Magic Thinking

AFTER A DHARMA TALK at the Cambridge Zen Center, a graduate student once asked Zen Master Seung Sahn, "I wanted to ask you a question that I've been told you probably won't consider very important, but I wanted to ask it anyway. I've been told that you might be able to perform something that my thinking-mind would consider to be magical. And my thinking-mind would like to see something magical, so I was wondering if you might be able to perform that for me."

"Magic?" Dae Soen Sa Nim replied. "Ahhhh. Tonight I arrived here at the Cambridge Zen Center, and had some dinner. Very good taste. So I can speak to you now." (Laughter from the assembly.) "Understand?"

The student was silent.

"Ha ha ha ha! You don't understand what real magic is. So then I ask you, what kind of magic do you mean?"

"Well, something that my thinking mind would feel was not following the accepted laws of physics and nature."

"OK," Dae Soen Sa Nim responded. "I ask you: what is

your thinking mind? Please give it to me. Then I'll show you magic." (Laughter.)

"Well, I can't really do that."

"So you don't understand this thinking mind. How can you understand my magic? You don't understand your thinking mind, so you don't understand my magic. If you want to understand my magic, first you must understand your thinking. So what is your thinking?"

The student replied, "My thinking mind can understand magic."

" 'My thinking mind'? What is 'my thinking mind'? Who asked me the question? Who are *you*?! Show me, please."

The student persisted, waving his hands. "No, no. I asked you first."

"So I hit you thirty times, OK? What can you do?"

The student was silent for a moment, then said weakly, "I don't know."

"I hit you; you don't know. That's my magic."

What Is God?

A STUDENT SAID TO Zen Master Seung Sahn, "In order to be a correct, believing Christian, you have to believe in the difference between good and evil. How can you be a correct, believing Christian and at the same time practice Zen?"

"Do you understand what God is?" Dae Soen Sa Nim asked.

The student looked down. "Well, no."

"So, you don't understand. You say 'God, God, God, God.' Wonderful speech. But you don't have the faintest idea what this speech means! That is very interesting.

"I sometimes teach at the Abbey of Gethsemani, a Trappist monastery in Kentucky." Dae Soen Sa Nim continued. "That's where Thomas Merton used to live. The monks invite us back every year to lead retreats and give *kong-an* interviews. They chant our style, and we chant their style. Then we do meditation, *kong-an* interviews, formal meals, and Dharma talks. They have an old chant that says, 'The God who is pure emptiness / is created as form. / Becoming substance, the light and dark, / the stillness and the storm.' *The God who is pure emptiness is created as form.* So, God is pure emptiness. What is pure emptiness? The Bible says, 'Be still, and know that I am God.' How do you become still? That's a very important point. Stillness and true emptiness mean there is no speech or words. So it's already before thinking arises. If you are still, then you understand what is correct, what is freedom, what is love. Love means 'without conditions.' When you're holding your opinions and your conditions, you can't understand love. You can't understand God. You can't understand equality, or what is correct and not correct.

"Being still means putting it all down: don't make your opinions, conditions, or situation. Then you become stillness, this completely pure emptiness that is also God's substance. Then that mind is clear like space; clear like space is clear like a mirror: everything is reflected. Red comes before the mirror, red is reflected; white comes, white. Someone is happy, I am happy; someone is sad, then so am I. Someone is thirsty, give her water; someone is hungry, then give him food. That is truth, and the great function of truth. But first you must attain truth, and that means there is no correct or incorrect. You only reflect this world like a mirror, OK?"

The student said, "I think I understand what you're getting at, but . . ."

Zen Master Seung Sahn continued, "Jesus said, 'I am the Way, truth, and life.' That means, if you see truth, you can see God's and Jesus's original face. So I ask you, what is truth?"

The student said, "Well, from a Christian point of view, I would . . ."

"Don't make it complicated," Dae Soen Sa Nim replied. "I ask you a very simple question: what is truth?"

"I don't know. Maybe you want me to answer a certain way. I am not really a Buddhist, after all."

"Ha ha ha ha! Very complicated mind! You ask me, 'What is truth?'"

"OK," the student said. "What is truth?"

"The wall behind you is white. The carpet is green. Understand?"

"I think so, but . . ."

"Don't do so much thinking, OK? 'Be still, and know that I am God.' It's very simple: the wall is white: that is truth. The carpet is green: that is truth. That is true wisdom; it is not difficult. So practice, perceive your true self, and then you will soon understand."

Zen and World Peace

A STUDENT ONCE SAID to Zen Master Seung Sahn, "A friend of mine in the peace movement thinks that Zen meditation makes world peace. He said that sitting Zen takes away the conflict between good and bad, and so it makes world peace. I don't understand."

Zen Master Seung Sahn replied, "Very few people can clearly perceive their mental power. It is like a magnet. We cannot see its power. But if you take two magnets, and try to push the 'plus' poles together, they will push away; if you push the 'minus' poles together, they will also repel each other. Even a much, much bigger magnet cannot attract a smaller magnet when the same poles are lined up.

"Our minds are just like that. When you start practicing, you don't understand your center. You cannot understand this mental power you have. But it's still there, even if you can't see it or feel it. It is not special.

"World peace is very simple. It only means your mental power coming into harmony with everyone else's, with this world. Then some balance appears. That is all. But first it means you must make harmony with yourself. Nowadays, many people argue for world peace. They want to make world peace in the outside world, but inside they have strong 'I like, I don't like' minds. They are very, very attracted to some things, and very, very repulsed by other things. All of this comes from the energy they make in their minds, which is not harmonious. So they cannot make world peace. All these world peace people cannot make world peace this way, because even they are always fighting each other. 'World peace must be this way!' 'No, it must be that way!' That is already not a peaceful mind! I think you understand this kind of mind.

"So our practice means cutting off all of this thinking. Don't make good and bad. We have a famous Zen question that asks, 'What is your original face?' That is a question about attaining our original mental power. There are two or three kinds of mental power. Actually, there are many different kinds, but here we will talk about three: opposites mental power, good mental power, and bad mental power. Christian teaching is all about original and absolute powers in total conflict, always fighting. You understand history, right? In the old-style history, evil forces and good forces are always fighting, fighting, fighting. Even Christian groups are always fighting with each other: 'I have the correct way! You are wrong!' 'No, mine is the true way!' Politics and social studies also concern themselves exclusively with this: what is positive to some groups, what is negative. Which things are good, and which things are bad. All of this is opposites. It cannot be fixed, and it cannot really fix anything else.

"Buddhism teaches that good and bad don't have any self-nature, so good and bad don't matter. Our focus is, what is your original, primary point? That is the Middle Way. If you find your original mental power, you can control both good and bad power. Then good and bad power become harmonious. Here's my left hand; that's my left hand. The right hand sometimes doesn't like the left hand. The left hand sometimes doesn't like the right hand. Then they're always fighting each other, so they cannot do anything together. But if your center becomes strong, then the left hand and right hand only follow your instructions: 'Bring that glass here!'

"But maybe the left hand is injured. Then you may say to it, 'Bring that glass here,' and the left hand may say, 'I'm in pain. I can't.' Then you say, 'Right hand, you go over and bring that here.' And the right hand says, 'No, that's not my job!' Then the left hand and right hand start fighting. That means your center is not strong; a lazy mind appears. The glass is over there, but the left hand is in pain, has had some accident or something, and it cannot pick up the glass. And the right hand says, 'I don't like that!' You say to it, 'OK, don't worry.' Then you sleep, so that you don't have to deal with this difficulty. This is how a lazy mind appears, because you have no center, OK?

"When you have a strong center, you can control this right and left hand. When your center is strong, good and bad already disappear. That's our absolute energy, absolute mental power. So this means, any time a good situation or condition appears, make it a correct action, which benefits other sentient beings. When a bad situation, feeling, or condition appears, also make it correct. That's the Middle Way. That's the point of most of the ancient Asian wisdom teaching style, OK? Taoism, Confucianism, and Buddhism all say something about mental power and the Middle Way. But Western philosophies nearly always have no Middle Way. Good or bad—which one? So they're always fighting.

"Correct meditation means finding our true self, our mental energy. Finding our true mental energy means having no good, no bad. Then correct mind-waves appear. Practice good, then good waves appear; practice bad, bad waves appear. Cut good and bad, then original waves appear. *Original waves* means universal waves: our waves are the same waves. So only put down everything, only go straight, don't know. Then your original waves and original energy and Middle Way energy come together, because the cycles are the same. So coming together is possible.

"Now, someone may ask, 'How can you prove that?' I answer, 'What color is the sky?' 'Blue.' 'Is that good or bad?' 'Not good, not bad: it's just blue.' 'Correct.' When you see the sky, it's just blue. That mind is already original nature. Original energy. That's enough. But most of us are holding our opinions, our conditions, and our situations: 'I don't like blue, I like gray.' People only make good and bad, so this world has good and bad, and there isn't world peace. But good and bad have no self-nature; only thinking makes good and bad. So don't make good and bad. Only practice, and then you can help this world, OK?"

The student bowed. "Thank you very much."

Keeping Not-Moving Mind

A STUDENT ASKED Zen Master Seung Sahn, "How can I keep my mind from moving when certain situations or conditions arise?"

"Where is your mind?" he replied. "Please give it to me."

The student did not respond.

"If you have no mind, then moving or not moving don't matter. You have mind, so it's moving. Please give me your mind. Where is your mind? Right now, where is it?"

The student still could not respond.

"Already not moving! Ha ha ha ha! You already gave me your mind. So you have no mind now. If you make your mind, it is always moving. If you don't make mind, there is nothing that is ever moving. 'My mind does this, my mind does that.' Nowadays you always hear people talking like this. That is very strange, yah? Originally, mind does not exist; you cannot find it anywhere. It is like last night's dream. When you have the dream, you think the dream and everything in it are real, and this affects you. But the moment you wake up, you see that the dream never really existed. You *think* that the

91

dream is real, and moving, but actually it is only thinking; that is all."

The student said, "But it always seems so real. I mean, it always comes and goes . . ."

Zen Master Seung Sahn continued, "Yah, if you make mind, then mind always seems to be moving. But really, where is your mind? Please give it to me."

"But I . . ." The student could not continue.

"You could not find your mind, yah? So you make your mind, and then you have a problem. Don't make your mind. You don't understand, so only go straight, don't know, OK? *Don't know* is very important. 'What am I?' *Don't know* . . . 'Where is my mind?' *Don't know* . . . 'When I was born, where did I come from?' *Don't know* . . . 'When I die, where do I go?' *Don't know* . . . Actually, you really *don't* know, in the deepest, most fundamental sense. That is a very important point to look into.

"If you keep don't-know mind, your mind has already disappeared. Don't-know mind already cuts off all thinking. *Cuts off all thinking* means no thinking. *No thinking* means empty mind. *Empty mind* means your nature *before* thinking arises. Before thinking, there is no mind. When thinking appears, mind appears. When mind appears, dharma appears. When dharma appears, form appears. And when any kind of form appears, then suffering appears: life and death, happiness and unhappiness, good and bad, like and dislike, coming and going. Mind disappears, dharma disappears. Dharma disappears, form disappears. Form disappears, then life and death, good and bad, happy and unhappy, coming and going—everything already disappears.

"So don't make mind, OK? Mind is only a name. People make names and forms, and attach to the names and forms, and don't see truth. So they suffer. (Holding up his Zen stick.) What is this? A stick, yah? But this stick never said, 'I am a stick.' Originally it has no name, but people make 'stick.' So its name is 'stick.' But it's not a stick. Only its *name* is 'stick.' So this is a stick, but it's not a stick.

"In the same way, your mind is not mind. You originally asked about your mind: you said 'mind' is moving. The name is mind. What is this name 'mind' *pointing* to? Do you understand that?

The student remained silent, looking at the floor.

"So don't be attached to the name—don't be attached to 'stick.' Do you understand that? Then (slamming the stick on the floor) you can perceive this stick's correct function."

Looking at the student who asked the question, Dae Soen Sa Nim asked, "So, in this sound (hitting the floor), is your mind moving or not moving?"

The student hit the floor.

"Correct! Wonderful! Only keep this mind. That's your true self."

Why Is the Sky Blue?

A STUDENT HAD THE following exchange with Zen Master Seung Sahn following a talk in St. Petersburg: "Zen Master, I ask you to check my mind and give me some advice."

"That's a very good question," Dae Soen Sa Nim replied. "Give me your mind. I'll take it away for you."

The student hit the floor.

"Why do you hit the floor? When you hit the floor, already your *I-my-me* mind disappears. Then how can you ask about mind?"

The student hit the floor again.

"You understand one, but you don't understand two."

"'You' and 'I,'" the student replied.

"You're attached to 'you' and 'I.'"

"No, I'm not," the student said.

"'No'? You're attached to *no*. You don't understand *no*."

The student did not respond.

"Why is the sky blue?" Dae Soen Sa Nim asked.

Pausing, the student replied, "Because the floor is yellow."

"No, I asked, 'Why is the sky blue?' I didn't ask you about the floor."

The student was silent.

"If you understand why the sky is blue, then you understand your true self. That's the point. Why is the sky blue? Why did you come into this world?"

The student replied, "What do you want?"

"I already hit you thirty times. Do you understand that? Not bad, not bad. Someone asked Zen Master Joju, 'Does a dog have Buddha-nature?' He said, '*Mu!*' ['No!'] So I ask you, what does *Mu* mean?"

"*Mu* means I hit Joju in the morning," the student replied.

"I asked you about *Mu*. Don't say anything about Joju, OK? What does *Mu* mean?"

"There is no dog, and no *Mu*."

"Don't explain it, OK? Too much thinking! You must cut your understanding; only keep don't-know."

The student hit the floor again.

Dae Soen Sa Nim replied, "That's only a sound, hitting the floor. You don't understand just *Mu*."

"I understand, I understand," the student protested. "I only . . ."

"Your thinking is a little complicated, yah? You must put down all of your thinking, only return to don't-know mind. Then your center will become stronger, stronger, stronger. OK? Very wonderful, this practicing. But one more step is necessary. Our practice means understanding our true self: *What am I?* Only keep a don't-know mind: 'What am I? *Don't know* . . .' Then your center becomes stronger and stronger. Your small 'I' disappears, then you attain nothing-I, you pass nothing-I, and you attain big-I: the whole universe is you, you are the universe. We call that *primary point.* Everything comes from primary point and returns to primary point. In your practice, this primary point will grow, grow, grow, grow, until you experience the true reality that, in fact, you and everything are never separate. The sky is blue, the tree is green, the dog is barking, 'Woof! Woof!' Sugar is sweet. When you see, when you hear, when you smell, when you taste, when you touch—everything is *just like this,* truth. You and truth are never separate.

"Then one more step is necessary: how do you make this truth function to make a correct life? This means, moment to moment, keep Great Love, Great Compassion: How help all beings? The name for this is the *Great Bodhisattva Way.*"

Who Made *You*?

A STUDENT IN Moscow asked Zen Master Seung Sahn, "What does Zen have to say about the social and economic problems in society? I mean, these are real things that we must worry about."

"Where does society come from? Where do economics come from? Do you understand that?"

The student was silent for a moment, and said, "Well, there can be many points of view on this—"

"Yah, that means, everything comes from thinking. Human beings make economics and society. Our thinking makes economics, and our thinking makes society. And because people attach to their thinking, they also attach to their different ideas about economics and society, and cannot agree at all. Soon fighting appears, and suffering. That is the usual style for most people.

"But Zen is not concerned with this. Rather, who makes this thinking? Who is thinking about economics? Who is thinking about society? *Who* is thinking? What am I? *Don't know . . .* That is already *before* thinking. Society and economics are after

97

thinking. But my true nature is *before* thinking arises. Attaining that is Zen. When you attain that, then your economic function can help other beings, and your social function can help other beings. But first you must attain your true self.

"Everything comes from a primary cause, combining with a condition, and then a result appears. If you attain the primary cause in your mind, and have some insight into the condition, then you attain the nature of this result. If you attain the result, how do you change your condition? How do you take away the primary cause? When you can do that, then everything is no problem. First, understand primary cause, and condition, and result. So I ask you, why did you come into this world?"

"Because my parents gave life to me," the student replied.

"Your parents? Your parents came from where? God made them?"

"They came from my grandparents."

"Grandparents came from where?"

The student could not respond.

"What is the primary cause?"

"The Absolute is the primary cause. The Absolute is that which cannot be named. You can't say directly what it is. It's that which can't be described."

Dae Soen Sa Nim burst out laughing, "Ha ha ha ha! If you cannot name the Absolute, why do you open your mouth so much? Your Absolute is too noisy! (Laughter from the assembly.) This is the mistake of a merely intellectual view of *anything.* That is why it says in the Bible, 'Be still, and know that I am God.' Being still means not giving rise to any thinking whatsoever; then the Absolute appears clearly. We call this 'only don't know.'

"But if you're thinking, even so much as to think or to say

WHO MADE *YOU?*

the word 'Absolute,' you already lose the true Absolute. Your thinking makes opposites, dualism. If you attain the Absolute, you attain everything. The Absolute means there are no opposites, no high and low, no coming or going, no speech and words. Opening your mouth is already a big mistake. So what can you do?"

The student persisted. "I can make mistakes, but what I want to say is . . ."

"Ha ha ha ha! You still like your thinking too much! Ha ha ha! (Laughter from the assembly.) So I ask you, very strongly, what are you? What are *you?*"

"A human being."

"What is a human being?"

The student could not answer.

"That's the point. You must attain your true self. Then you will attain everything."

The student continued to talk over him.

"If you open your mouth, you only make more and more and more mistakes. So practicing Zen means finding this primary cause. The primary cause, the Absolute, has nothing whatsoever to do with your thinking. So even attempting to use one word to express it is a mistake.

"A long time ago, Shakyamuni Buddha was staying at Yong Sahn Mountain. Over a thousand people were gathered to hear him speak. Everyone was very excited. They asked each other, 'What kind of Dharma speech will he give?' 'What will he have to say to us today?' The Buddha sat down, and the crowd became very quiet, waiting for his Dharma speech. One minute passed, and the Buddha did not say anything. Two more minutes passed. Three minutes. But the Buddha did not open his mouth. Maybe ten minutes passed. Finally, he reached down, picked a flower, and lifted it over his head. Nobody

99

understood—only Mahakashyapa smiled. Then the Buddha said, 'I give my true Dharma Transmission to you.'

"The Buddha only picked up a flower: what does this mean? What does Mahakashyapa's smile mean?"

The student was now silent.

"Yah, don't understand! Ha ha ha ha! If you attain that point, you attain your true self. You attain the correct way, truth, and correct life. Jesus said, 'I am the way, the truth, and the life.' Zen says the same thing: find your true self, find truth, find the correct way. Christians depend on God to find this. Zen means not depending on *anything.* Our direction is 'What am I?' Only *don't know,* 100 percent.

"Some people think that this 'not-knowing mind' is some mysterious Buddhist state of mind. A long time ago, Socrates used to walk all around Athens, in the markets and the plazas, only saying, 'You must understand yourself! You must understand yourself!' But nobody understood what he meant. So one of his younger students asked him, 'Teacher, do you understand *your* true self?' 'No, I don't know my true self,' Socrates replied, 'But I understand this not-knowing.' So this don't-know mind is very important. It is not Eastern or Western, Buddhist or Christian.

"So, the Buddha picked up a flower: nobody understands. That's don't-know mind. Some eighteen hundred years ago, Bodhidharma went to China, and eventually met the emperor. The emperor said to him, 'I have built many temples, fed and clothed many monks. How much merit have I earned?' Bodhidharma said, 'None.' The emperor became very angry. 'Who are you?' he demanded. Bodhidharma only replied, 'Don't know.' Then Bodhidharma went to a place above Shaolin Temple, and sat in a cave facing the wall for over nine years. Only go straight—don't know.

"Socrates' don't-know mind, the Buddha's don't-know mind, Bodhidharma's don't-know mind, your don't-know mind, my don't-know mind, everybody's don't-know mind is the same don't-know mind. When you are born, where do you come from? When you die, where do you go? Who are *you*? *DON'T KNOW*. That's the point.

"So don't-know mind is very important. When you are thinking, your mind and my mind are different. When you cut off all thinking, your mind and my mind are the same. If you keep a don't-know mind 100 percent, then your don't-know mind, my don't-know mind, Socrates' don't-know mind, the Buddha's don't-know mind is all the same mind. Don't-know mind cuts off all thinking: there's no thinking, which is already *before* thinking. Your before-thinking is your substance and my before-thinking is my substance—which is this flower's substance and universal substance and everything's substance. If you keep this don't-know mind 100 percent, at that time, already you are the universe, the universe is you. You and everything already become one. We call that *primary point* (hits the table with his Zen stick).

"But don't know is not 'don't know,' some *thing*; don't know is primary point. Primary point's *name* is don't know. Everything comes from primary point and returns to primary point. Somebody may say that this primary point is mind, or God, or Buddha, or the Absolute, or energy, or nature, or substance, or holiness, or consciousness, or self, or soul, or everything. But this primary point is already before thinking. So there is no name and no form for it, no speech or words for it, because this point is before thinking (hits the table with his Zen stick). When you keep don't-know mind 100 percent, you and everything already become one. That is Zen mind. Only go straight don't know, then you and everything become one.

"Keeping a don't-know mind 100 percent, you and every-thing already are one. At that time, this stick, this sound (hit-ting the table), and your mind—are they the same or different?"

Someone shouted from the back of the hall, "Yes, same." Someone else shouted, "They're different."

Dae Soen Sa Nim replied, "Same? Different? If you say 'same,' this stick will hit you thirty times. If you say 'different,' this stick will also hit you thirty times. (Hitting the table.) That's *before* thinking. It has no speech or words. Opening your mouth is already a mistake. Close your mouth, and how do you answer? That's the point. It's not special, it's not magic. Only keep a don't-know mind, then you understand this point.

"This sound's substance (hitting the table), your mind's substance, this stick's substance, universal substance, energy substance are all the same substance. This substance is all be-fore thinking, so words and names cannot touch it. It's very easy. So opening your mouth is not necessary. Same or differ-ent? Answering that question is very simple. Too much under-standing means too many problems. If you don't know, then no problem. Ha ha ha! So only go straight don't know, then you can digest your understanding and it becomes wisdom.

"Everybody I meet here in Russia is very smart, maybe *too* smart. But intellectual understanding means having someone else's idea, not your idea. When you are young, someone teaches you, 'The sky is blue,' and your whole life you go around saying, 'The sky is blue,' 'The sky is blue,' 'The sky is blue.' That is very interesting! Ha ha ha ha! But this sky never says, 'I am blue.'

"Everybody says, 'The sky is blue,' or 'The tree is green,' or 'The dog barks, "Woof! Woof!"'" Somebody taught you to believe 'The sky is blue,' and so you believe 'The sky is blue.' But these are all just ideas, other people's ideas, which are all different from each other. Korean people say, 'The dog barks, "Mung! Mung! Mung!"' Japanese people say, 'The dog barks, "Wong! Wong! Wong!"' Polish people say, 'The dog barks, "How! How! How!"' American people say, 'The dog barks, "Woof! Woof!"' All people have different sounds, and all have different ideas. But this barking dog never gives his sound a name; he only barks. Human beings make this word and sound, an idea, and become attached to it. Then they cannot see this world as it is.

"What is before words and sound? That means, what is *before* thinking? Zen means finding this before-thinking, this primary point. If you attain this point, you attain everything."

Abortion

SOMEONE ASKED Zen Master Seung Sahn in Warsaw, "Nowadays in Poland, there is much fighting over the issue of abortion. Many people say that a woman and her doctor should go to jail if they commit an abortion. Other people say that nothing should happen to them, because it is a woman's right to have this done, it is her conscience. I don't understand. As a Zen student, what is correct?"

Zen Master Seung Sahn replied, "Buddhism's first moral precept is a very strong one: do not take any life. And at the same time, Zen Buddhism also guides us to the absolute insight that any action is fundamentally not good, not bad. So for many people, this can seem confusing. But actually it is very simple.

"The most important thing to consider when doing any action is, *why* do you do something? Only for you, or for all beings? Why do you eat every day—only for your body, for your tongue's pleasure? If your direction is clear, then any action is clear. If your direction is not clear, even doing 'good' actions every day is not always clear. *Correct direction* means your actions are already beyond good and bad, and not based on the false notion of 'I.' So what kind of direction do you have? Why would you abort this baby? Determining that clearly in your mind is most important."

The student persisted. "But soon there will be a referendum on this issue. If it becomes a law, then you can go to jail for having an abortion."

Dae Soen Sa Nim replied, "Whether or not you go to jail is not the way to decide this. The only thing that must be clear is why or why not you would have this abortion. Why does this doctor help? If the direction of this act is clear, everything is clear. If your direction is not clear, everything is not clear. Buddhism is not only about human beings. It is a teaching pointing to the substance of all beings. Even one blade of grass is valuable: remember, the first precept is don't kill *any* life. Of course this baby is a human being. Yet if necessary, killing the Buddha, eminent teachers, and Zen masters is no problem. They are also living beings. That is Buddhism.

"We have five precepts: don't kill life, don't lie, don't steal, don't misuse intoxicants, and don't misuse sexual relations. In the mountains, a man is collecting firewood. A rabbit runs by, and runs to the left. A few minutes later, a hunter runs by, carrying a gun, and asks, 'Which way did the rabbit go?' If the man makes correct speech, and doesn't lie, the hunter will find the rabbit and kill it. If the man strictly keeps the precept of not lying—simply for the sake of keeping precepts, to be a 'good' Buddhist who does no wrong—the rabbit will suffer, and the hunter will suffer, too. For by the law of cause and effect, the hunter will have to reap some effect from his actions, in this life or the next.

"But if your direction for keeping the precepts is truly to liberate all beings from suffering, then you will maybe tell a lie: 'Oh, the rabbit went that way,' pointing away from the direction where the rabbit really ran. This hunter will not find the rabbit, and the rabbit will live. These five precepts include not killing and not lying. At that time, break the precepts or keep them? Which one?"

The student answered, "I prefer that he does not catch this rabbit."

"Of course. That's Buddhism. Our teaching says that you must not kill, especially human beings. But when a bad man comes and hurts many people, a policeman sometimes kills that person. But this policeman is not killing for himself, because of his own angry mind. His action of killing is to save sentient beings from suffering.

"There is another way to look at this. I always talk about the fact that nowadays there are too many human beings in this world. In 1945, there were two billion people on this planet. By the year 2000 there were over six billion people. In twenty more years, there will be eight billion people. In India, meanwhile, many people have no food, no clothes, no house. Every day, between seven and eight thousand people die from one or two diseases alone. Every day. No food, no clothes, no house. Babies are suffering. Why make all this suffering for babies? America is an example of a country with a good situation, and perhaps you could say that in most parts of the United States, babies don't suffer so much, and having babies is no problem. But in poor countries, babies have so many problems. So what can you do?

"Nowadays most big animals have almost died out. Tigers, elephants, whales are all disappearing. Five years from now, they will be nearly all gone. Human beings make such a problem in this world. So all human beings must wake up, very soon! That is a very important point. If human beings do not wake up very soon, this world will soon collapse.

"So, whether or not babies should be born is not the point. Instead, what is human beings' correct direction? It is very important to find that. Some two thousand five hundred years ago, the Buddha taught, 'Don't kill any life.' That is the Buddha's teaching. But the behind-meaning means having Great Love, Great Compassion, and the Great Bodhisattva Way. It is extremely important that this not be considered as simply a question of whether or not to have a baby, or whether abortion is 'good' or 'bad.'

"Rather, we must deeply consider what is human beings' correct direction and correct way, right now? At *this* time? How does this action help other beings? Find that, and moment to moment to moment, just do it. If you find that, any action, situation, or condition doesn't matter. You must do it. That is Great Love. That is Great Compassion. The name for that is the Great Bodhisattva Way.

What to Do about Sleeping

A STUDENT ASKED Zen Master Seung Sahn, "When I sit in meditation, I always sleep. This is a big problem. What can I do about it?"

Dae Soen Sa Nim replied, "A long time ago in Korea, there was a Zen monk who only slept in the Dharma room, during meditation. He would hear the sound of the wooden *chukpi* signaling the beginning of a meditation period, and would immediately fall asleep. If he didn't hear the *chukpi,* he wouldn't fall asleep. That is very strange karma, yah?

"One day, the head monk could no longer tolerate the constant snoring during meditation, and called the sleeping monk to his room. 'You're a real rockhead. You don't belong in the meditation hall. You need to find some other place to sleep!' So the monk left the Dharma room. As he was walking away, the head monk hit the *chukpi* inside the meditation hall, to begin another round of sitting, and this monk fell asleep even while walking! All he needed to do was hear this *chukpi* sound, and no matter what, he fell asleep. It was very humiliating for him!

"So finally the monk had a good idea: he gathered some heavy rocks, and carried them with him as he did walking meditation around the yard. He walked all day, no matter what. Whenever sleep appeared, these rocks fell to the ground—*boom!*—waking him up. So that was this monk's practice: walking, walking, walking. 'Be careful, be careful, be careful,' he reminded himself. After many months of this kind of practice, one day he heard the sound of the *chukpi* from the meditation hall, signaling the end of sitting: *slap! slap! slap!* Upon hearing that, the monk's mind opened, and he got enlightenment. Then the rocks all fell down! 'I got big rocks!' he shouted. The temple's Zen master saw that and began laughing, 'The rockhead got enlightenment.'

"So, sleeping is a big demon. But if you work with it, instead of just following it or fighting with it, then this sleeping karma can help you. One of my old students also had heavy sleeping karma. Every sitting period, only sleep, sleep, sleep. Then one day I told him to put a roll of toilet paper on his head, and keep his breathing energy in his center. Whenever he nodded off, the toilet paper would fall down and make a sound, which everyone in the Dharma room could hear. So this really made the monk embarrassed, because everyone in the room could tell when he fell asleep, even those with their backs to him on the opposite side of the room! And what is more, he only realized for the first time how much he was falling asleep by doing this kind of practice.

"So the monk really began to try much, much harder. And eventually, after several months of practicing like this, he reached deep inside and somehow, through great effort and paying attention, he overcame his sleeping demons. So you must perceive your sleeping-mind. It's a very good teacher, even better than a Zen master. If you try very hard, you will perceive this. This is how you can fight sleep."

The student bowed and said, "Thank you for your teaching."

Cinema Zen

A STUDENT ASKED Zen Master Seung Sahn, "I have heard this teaching about cutting off thinking, inside and outside becoming one, and believing in my true self. I have heard this so many times, but I don't know if it is possible for me. How can I believe in my true self 100 percent? It seems so difficult."

"Very easy! Do you have ten dollars? I will show you for ten dollars!" (Laughter from the assembly.)

"Ten dollars? But what does that have to do with—"

"Only buy a movie ticket! Ha ha ha ha!" (Loud, extensive laughter from the assembly.) When you go to the movies, what kind of mind do you have then?"

"I just watch."

"Just watch? So you can already believe your eyes. You can believe your ears. That means you can believe in your true self. Inside and outside already become one. Before the movie, your habit-mind is always checking, checking, checking. After the movie, your mind returns to thinking, thinking, thinking. But while you watch this movie, there is no thinking. Have you ever seen *Star Wars*? Spaceships flying through the sky, many bombs exploding, the good guys chasing the bad men. At that time, you are only 'Ahhh! That's *wonderful*!!' When someone in the movie is happy, you become happy. When someone becomes sad, you also become sad. You and the movie become one; there is no inside and no outside. At that time, during the movie, there is no thinking. You are not planning for tomorrow, or regretting yesterday. There are no random thoughts to follow. Only—*boom!*—you become one with the action in this movie: it can make you laugh or cry or feel angry.

"So, watching a movie is true Zen mind. At that time, you believe in your true self 100 percent. After the movie, thinking appears, and you suffer. You fall back into believing the movie in your head. Ha ha ha ha! (Laughter from the assembly.) So, if you still don't believe in your true self 100 percent, you must go to the movies all day, every day. (Laughter.) Then no problem, OK?"

"OK!"

Killing Plants

A STUDENT ASKED Zen Master Seung Sahn, "If the Buddha said, 'Don't kill anything,' why don't you teach about not killing plants?"

Dae Soen Sa Nim replied, "One day, the monks of the Eastern Hall and the Western Hall were fighting over a cat. Each group believed that the temple cat belonged to them. 'That is our cat!' 'No, that is *our* cat!' Fighting, fighting, fighting. Zen Master Nam Cheon heard the commotion, went out, and picked up the cat by its scruff. In the other hand, he wielded a large, sharp knife. 'If any one of you can say one meaningful word, I will save this cat. If you cannot, I will kill it!' The monks were dumbfounded; nobody could say anything! Then Master Nam Cheon promptly sliced the cat in two.

"This is a number-one bad action! But killing or not killing doesn't matter. Why kill something? Why not kill something? Having a clear direction about your life is very important. If your direction is clear, killing and not killing are no problem. If your direction is clear, then even if the Buddha appears, you must kill the Buddha. If bodhisattvas appear, you must kill the bodhisattvas. If any Zen masters appear, you must kill the Zen masters. Demons appear? Kill! Zen Master Seung Sahn appears? No problem—only *kill*. (Laughter.) If you kill everything, then you get enlightenment, big enlightenment. If you don't kill anything, then you can't get enlightenment."

"But I meant something else," the student said. "Everybody knows that eating meat is no good because we have to kill animals in order to eat them. But nobody says anything about killing plants in order to eat them."

"If necessary, then even eating the Buddha is no problem. (Laughter.) You want to hear me tell you that doing such-and-such is good, or doing such-and-such is bad. But that is not Zen style. Rather, how much is your action based on insight into your true nature? How much does your kind of action help all beings? *That* is most important.

"One of my students sent me a letter, in which he wrote, 'Zen Master, I have a problem. You sent me a picture of Shakyamuni Buddha. I kept it on my desk. My one-year-old son climbed up onto the table and ate the Buddha. What should I do?' I sent him a letter saying, 'Your baby is stronger than Buddha, and is a great Zen master. He has no hindrance. You must learn everything from your son, then you will soon get enlightenment.' (Much laughter.)

"So, what is Buddha? Eating vegetables, eating meat isn't the whole point. Only: *why* do that? Attaining this direction is very important. I already talked about the great Zen Master Nam Cheon. Then there is National Teacher Hae Chung, who refused to kill any of the grass that was used to bind him to the ground by a group of thieves. One monk killed a cat, and became a great Zen master. Another monk kept the precepts so strictly that he wouldn't kill even one blade of grass, and became a great national teacher in China. Which one do you like? (Laughter from the assembly.)

"So you must always be clear about why you do something, whether killing or giving life. That is the Zen way. If it becomes necessary, you must even be able to kill the Buddha. If not necessary, you must not kill even a single blade of grass."

Zen Master in Love

A STUDENT ASKED Zen Master Seung Sahn, "In your life, have you ever been deeply in love with a woman?"

"Of *course*! (Loud laughter from the assembly.) All beautiful ladies are in my mind. Never separate, all the time."

"Was there ever one lady, one very special woman who would really take your mind, I mean really steal your heart?" (Laughter.)

"One lady? Yes. Do you want to know who?"

"Yes, if you can, please," the student responded.

"Kwan Seum Bosal!* Ha ha ha ha! (Loud, sustained laughter from the assembly.) She's a very beautiful lady! Beautiful face, beautiful necklace, beautiful clothes. Beautiful lady! (Laughter.) Do you like her, too?"

---

*Kwan Seum Bosal (Kuan Yin in Chinese, Kannon in Japanese), the Bodhisattva of Compassion, is usually depicted in female form, adorned with precious jewels.

Karma Talking

A STUDENT ASKED Zen Master Seung Sahn, "I often hear people talk about karma. Is that what is meant when people speak about merit? People who gave money to monks in the old days, or built *stupas* or temples, or chanted or practiced—in Buddhist tradition, they get merit for these activities. What is merit, and what is karma?"

Dae Soen Sa Nim replied, "A long time ago in China, during the Yang Dynasty, the emperor invited the national teacher, a famous Zen master, to the palace. 'I am the emperor,' he said to the monk. 'What kind of karma did I have before I was born as the emperor?'

"The Zen master perceived his mind for a few moments, and said, 'In a previous life, you were the son of two poor people. Your parents had very little food. So every day you went to the mountains to gather firewood for sale in the town. You gave the money to your parents, because they were very old and sick. You did this every day, without fail. You only stayed in the woods and the mountains, so you had a very pure mind. There was a cave on the trail that went up the mountain, and in front of this cave was a stone Buddha. Every time you passed it, you would stop and bow. Even if you were carrying a big bundle of wood, you would stop, set down the bundle, and bow very deeply before picking up the bundle again and resuming your way.

"'One day, while you were carrying some firewood down from the mountain, it started to rain very hard. When you reached the cave, you saw the Buddha statue getting wet in the cold rain. You became very sad, and thought, 'How can I help the Buddha?' So you took off a large hat you were wearing and put it on the Buddha, to keep its head dry. The next day, you built a little cabin around the statue so that it would always be shielded from the rain, wind, and snow. This action brought you a lot of merit, because this simple action indicated clearly how much you only thought of helping other people. Many years later, when you died, you were reborn as the emperor of China in this life. So it is always very important to have this kind of mind.'

"When the old Zen master finished telling the story, the emperor smiled. He was very happy. His wife was sitting nearby, and overhead the whole story. She felt not a little jealous to hear the pious roots of her husband's good fortune, and wished to hear from what bright deeds her own high station had sprung. 'Zen master,' she asked, 'What is my previous life's karma?'

"The Zen master hesitated for a moment, and said, 'I cannot tell you.'

"'Why not? I want to know!'

"'Your past life was very strange. I cannot say anything.'

"'No, no, no, I want to know about my previous life,' she said. 'Please tell me!'

"'I cannot.'

"But the emperor's wife persisted. 'Please, tell me any-thing. Any kind of speech is no problem.'

"After a short pause, the Zen master said, 'OK, any kind of speech I'll tell you. But don't be angry with me if you don't like it.'

"'No problem,' she replied. 'But please, tell me every-thing.'

"'In your past life, you were a worm. You used to live in the ground in front of a great precepts temple. From time to time, you would stick your head up out of the ground to listen to the chanting in the temple, or sometimes to hear the sound of the great temple bell and drum.

"'In the temple lived Do Soen Sunim, a highly revered precepts master. In his entire life, he never committed a single bad action. Only correct, correct, every day. One day, he was out cutting some of the grass in front of the temple with a great big scythe. Soon the temple drum was sounded, and you poked your head up out of the grass to hear it. *Swishhhhhh-hhh!!*—Do Soen Sunim's scythe cut through the grass, lopping off your head. When Do Soen Sunim saw what he had done, he became very upset. He bowed deeply, and said the mantra *Namu Amita Bul, Namu Amita Bul, Namu Amita Bul* seven times. You were then reborn as a woman who became the emperor's wife.'

"'I was a worm?! That's not possible. You are lying!'

"'If you don't believe me,' the Zen master said, 'Then why don't you find out for yourself?'

"'How?'

"'If you do strong meditation practice, you will be able to perceive your own past-life karma.'

"The emperor's wife was so angry, she decided to do just that, if only to prove this monk wrong and erase the embarrassment of his words. Every morning without fail, she awoke early and began meditating. It was very hard training. One morning, she had a breakthrough—*psshhhewww!!*—and her karma became clear. She saw that the great national teacher had not been lying to her. 'In my past life, I was a worm,' she thought to herself. 'It's true, every day I listened to that bell sound, and the beating of the drum, and the sound of the monks chanting. And yes, one day that precepts master killed me, and chanted *Namu Amita Bul* seven times over my body. That was only a small amount of merit, but I still became the emperor's wife in this life.'

"So in this life cause and effect are very clear. Everybody gathered here was a very good Zen student in his or her past life. That is why you are here today. If you just practice, and don't be attached to your condition, your situation, or problems, everybody will soon get enlightenment, become great bodhisattvas, and save all beings from suffering. That is the nature of merit, what is sometimes called, in other situations, karma.

"A dog has dog karma. A cat has cat karma. A snake has snake karma. And human beings have human karma. Animals only understand their own karma: a dog only barks, and does not make cat sounds. Also, dogs do not become involved with the actions of cats, and vice versa. Animals have only action.

"But human beings have thinking, so they make many different kinds of karma, some of it very complex, and they hold on to that karma. Then they don't understand their correct job, so they fight, kill each other in order to get money, get fame, get power, and also kill animals for food and pleasure, and pollute the earth, air, and water. So they must return to their true self, where there is no I-my-me mind. No I-my-me mind means the universe and I are not separate. This is world peace.

"There are three kinds of karma: correct karma, bad karma, and good karma. Correct karma is bodhisattva karma. Good karma means good habit. Bad karma means bad habit. Karma is only mind action, mind direction. If you attain the nature of your karma, your karma will reduce. Then you can use your karma to help other beings."

"Thank you very much for your teaching," the student said, bowing deeply.

You Are a Robot!

A man once asked Zen Master Seung Sahn, "What is sitting?"

"Sitting means keeping a not-moving mind. Do you have a mind?"

"Well, I think so."

"I think you have no mind. You're only a corpse. Why are you dragging this corpse around? That's very bad. If you say, 'I'm not a corpse,' then please give me one live word."

"Me," the man responded.

" 'Me?' "

"You."

"What is 'me'? What is 'you'?"

"That is all I can say about my self," the student said.

"You say 'me.' You say 'you.' But 'me' and 'you' are only names. What is 'me'? What is 'you'? Who is it that *says* those things?"

The student could not answer.

"So I say, you are a robot! (Laughter from the assembly.)

Have you ever seen *Star Wars*? There is a robot in this movie that can talk—it also says 'me' and 'you.' It says a lot of things, just like you. Yet this robot has no mind. So I think you also have no mind."

"But I do have a mind."

"You have a mind? Then please show it to me."

The man could not answer.

"You cannot even show me."

"Well, it's because, umm, I'm not sure what you teach."

"Zen teaching is very simple. Our Zen teaching is, you must find your mind. Where is your mind? (Pointing to his leg.) Is it here? (Pointing to belly.) Here? (Pointing to arm.) Here? (Pointing to head.) Here? Where is it?"

The man pointed to his head.

"How big is it?" Dae Soen Sa Nim asked. "What color? What shape is it? How big is your mind?"

"Very big."

"How big?" Zen Master Seung Sahn made various sizing gestures with his fingers and arms. "Is it this big, or this big, or this big? How big?"

But to each question, the man only responded, "Bigger." Finally, the man stretched his arms back as far as he could.

"Only that big? That's a very small mind. You think that's big, but you don't understand your mind. Your speech is all lies. Why are you deceiving everybody? Correct understanding is necessary. (Hits the table twice.) 'That is my mind!!' OK?"

The man just looked at the floor.

"You don't understand that? You still think, 'I have mind.' That is very wrong, and not true. It's a mistake. If you keep this mind, your whole life is a mistake. This is because mind is no-mind. (Holding up his stick.) What is this? It's a stick,

123

right? But this stick never said, 'I am a stick,' We say 'stick.' The name of this is 'stick.' But this thing never said, 'My name is stick.' The stars, the sun, the moon never called themselves these things. The sun never said 'I am sun.' The moon never said 'I am moon.' So true sun, true moon, true star, true stick, true mind have no names. All of these names are made by thinking.

"So you must understand, 'My mind is no-mind.' That's the first course. If you understand this first course, then the next course is seeing that 'mind' is not correct, and 'no-mind' is also not correct. We already showed how 'mind' is just a name; but if you are attached to speech and words, then 'no-mind' is also a name. So we say that opening your mouth is already a big mistake, because 'mind,' 'no-mind,' and everything else is made by thinking. If you cut off all thinking, there are no words and no speech. Cutting off all thinking means returning to your before-thinking mind. If you keep a before-thinking mind, then everything and you already become one. The sun, the moon, the stars, this stick, and your mind—everything—are already one, because before-thinking is your original substance. This substance, the star's substance, the moon's substance, universal substance is the same substance. We sometimes call that *primary point*. If you attain that primary point, then you get everything, because everything is already yours. You and the universe are never separate.

"Now, do you understand all that? It's very difficult, but also it's not difficult. Only try, try, try for ten thousand years. Keep a don't-know mind 100 percent—'What am I?' Don't *knowwww* . . . Not only this life, but for life after life after life after life after life, just keep this try-mind. Difficult, not difficult, getting enlightenment, not getting enlightenment don't matter. Only try. If you have try-mind, there is already no I-my-me. But if you make I-my-me, and hold I-my-me, you cannot find true Dharma, cannot find your true self, cannot find the true way. So put down your I-my-me, and only try, try, try for ten thousand years nonstop. That's very important. Then you will get everything."

The student bowed and said, "Thank you very much."

Your Nature Is Not Strong

A STUDENT AT THE Seoul International Zen Center once asked Zen Master Seung Sahn during a morning talk, "Sir, you always say that thinking is made by mind. And mind comes from our nature. Who makes our nature? We make our nature. But usually this nature is very strong. So how can we make it in the first place?"

Zen Master Seung Sahn replied, "Strong? How is nature strong? Who makes strong? Nature is empty, and originally nothing: that is 'strong?'"

"Well," the student replied, "When we haven't eaten for several days, then our nature is that we must eat."

"Your nature is never hungry, OK? Yes, your body may be hungry. But true nature is never hungry, never full."

"Well then, what exactly is our nature?"

Zen Master Seung Sahn responded, "Your lips are moving now. (Laughter from the assembly.) That is your nature. Don't make anything special about your 'nature.' Hungry-time, eat; thirsty-time, drink. That is all."

(Never) Finish Saving All Beings

A STUDENT ASKED, "An eminent teacher once said, 'I have already finished saving all beings from suffering.' I have also heard you say this once. What does this mean?"

"There is no end. Only try; don't check. If you are not checking anything, you have already finished saving all beings. If you have checking, you never finish. Which one do you like?"

The student bowed.

Zen, Astrology, Karma

WHEN ASKED ABOUT the meaning of astrology, Zen Master Seung Sahn taught his students as follows:

"There are many people who are interested in astrology. Every time such people make a decision or meet someone, they check their horoscope to see if something will be successful for them or not. In Korea and China, there are people who can read your face, or read your palm. If your eyebrows are like this, you have a strong mind. If they are like that, you have a weak mind. If you know the form, you can know the karma.

"It is like this: unripe fruit has a very beautiful color, but the taste is not very good. Slightly overripe fruit does not have a very beautiful color, perhaps even some spots, but the taste is very, very delicious. So understanding the form is very important if you want to understand the nature of this fruit's taste. If the form is very good, and the color is strong and clear, perhaps the fruit will not yet taste so good; but if the form and color are changed a certain way, you can understand something about the taste. So if you understand this form, you understand the nature of the taste. And if you understand your own form—your appearance, the way your thoughts are—then you can know something about your karma. You can understand your past karma, and you can understand your future karma. That is because karma is a kind of form, a kind of form of your life. The ways you form your thoughts become mind-habits, and those mind-habits become set as a kind of self-made rhythm underpinning and shaping your life. The name for that is karma. Thinking makes your karma, and this karma makes your body. Because we are attached to the condition of this body, our body-experience influences our thinking and karma. Karma makes your body—your physical form—and your body makes your karma. Around and around, nonstop.

"In Korea, there are astrologers who read your life on the basis of four numbers: the year, month, day, and time of your birth. If you understand these, then you can understand someone's past and future. In a way, you can say that this is mostly a kind of statistical understanding.

"One day a long, long time ago in China, a certain king wondered if, in a country so large, there might not be another person with the same four birth numbers as his. If so, then such a man must necessarily be king, like him. This king was often a little nervous, because he worried, 'Maybe there is someone out there who can replace me?'

"So he ordered the minister in charge of the national registry to check the lists of births and see if there might not be such a person who was born in the same year, and the same month, and at the same time on the same day. Lo and behold, it turned out that there was one man who had the same four numbers! This made the king even more nervous. But since the man lived deep, deep in the mountains, far from the capital city, the king got a little rest-mind.

"Then the king became very angry with the royal astrologer. 'You're no good! There is a man in our kingdom who has the same four numbers as I do, but he's not king. I am king! So your silly numbers do not determine things as you say they do. What have you been teaching me about this astrology business all these years?'

"But the royal astrologer was not afraid. He had studied for many, many years, under the best masters in the land. He knew that the numbers could not tell a lie. 'Your Highness, perhaps this other man has the same job.' This made the king even more nervous! So he immediately dispatched the royal court astrologer to the mountains to find this man who might be king!

"After several days of travel, the astrologer finally arrived in a tiny village deep in the mountains. When he found the man, he asked him, 'What is your job?'

" 'I have no job.'

" 'Then how do you eat?' the astrologer asked.

" 'Oh, I gather honey that the bees make.' Then the royal astrologer understood! Many, many bees work all day, make honey, and give it to the man, who then controls their lives. He had more or less the same job as the king after all!

"The astrologer immediately sped back to the capital city and the royal palace. He told the king, 'This man and you have the same job! Only the title is different. You are the king of this country, and he is the king of the bees' country. So it is the same job! His year is the same as yours, the month and day, too. But the time is very, very slightly different. So, you have a big job, and he has a smaller job. But the structure and function are basically the same.' The king was immediately relieved.

"This fortune-teller understood these men's karma by understanding the numbers related to their births. This karma is a kind of form. But form is emptiness. Who made this form? Who made the form that determines your life? Who made your karma?

"You made it. I make my karma; someone else makes their karma. Some primary cause arises in our minds and, following conditions, produces the same results. If you only go straight, practicing very hard—meditation, and especially chanting and bowing—your karma can be changed: you can control your karma's direction. It is very important that when you practice, you do not check 'good' feelings or 'bad' feelings. Then your karma will slowly, slowly disappear, and then your life will change. Then the fortune-tellers will no longer be correct.

"So how do you change your karma? We can sometimes explain it like this: Let us say that tomorrow someone will die. This is his karma, the result of the very subtle interplay of his thinking as it meets conditions. Maybe someone has seen his future and can tell that such-and-such accident will befall him the next day, leading to his death. Meanwhile he has started chanting, chanting, chanting, or doing strong mantra practice. Then the causes and conditions that are tending to lead him toward this accident start to not come together as well as when it was perceived that he was going to die. That is because, at the moment of the prediction of the death, this fortune-teller has seen the man's mind energy tending in a certain direction. If he just lives according to the energy that he has in his mind at that time, he cannot escape the meeting of energies that is his death. But chanting 'straightens out' the karma—the mind energy—and it leads to a slightly different result: he gets in an accident, but ends up only breaking his leg. He does not die after all! This is possible.

"Karma is only made by thinking. My style thinking makes my karma; your style thinking makes your karma. If you can control your thinking, you can control somewhat the cause and effect that arises out of it. If I hit someone, I make bad karma. This person has a bad feeling and hits me back. I hit him again; he hits me again. Again and again and again: this is samsara, the wheel of cause and effect.

"But if the man I hit is a good man, he doesn't care. When I hit him, he only bows. Maybe he turns the other cheek. I hit him again; he only bows again. Then this is no longer interesting to me, so I stop. Then this samsara that I have been creating stops. He is only chanting to himself, or doing mantra practice. So his karma is already changing and his mind-light is shining into my mind. Instead of following the anger that may arise in his mind as a result of my hitting him, his practicing enables him to see that his anger is fundamentally empty. Also his thinking about his anger is empty, his judgment is empty, everything is empty and without self-nature. So it does not affect him; he does not attach to anything that arises in his mind, nor does he follow it. As a result, his karma is shining brightly into my mind, the same karma. So if you correctly save your true self, then it is possible to save your friends, your family, your fellow countrymen.

"If you practice hard, you can change your karma. If you do not practice hard, you cannot control your mind, cannot control your desire, anger, and ignorance. Then all of these things control you, and your life is only samsara. Your karma comes from samsara, and creates samsara, around and around and around. Then your four-number program is in total control of your life—what day this, what day that: it has all been decided.

"The most important thing is, how do you keep just-now

mind? If you correctly keep just-now mind, you can change your life. Everything before was largely determined by the karma you created in your own mind. But when you practice, your mind becomes empty, and you can change your life, moment to moment. This is why we practice."

Zen Master Seung Sahn
Remembers His Teacher

ZEN MASTER KO BONG was one of the great monks of the twentieth century. After all, he received *inka* from the great Zen Master Man Gong, and his one Dharma heir brought Korean Buddhism to the world. But even to many of his contemporaries, and now to history, precious little is known of this severe, enigmatic monk. He rarely gave public Dharma talks, and he did not accept students easily; those he did accept often had very little to say about his everyday life. He left behind no written records of his teaching.

In the mid-1980s, Zen Master Seung Sahn gave an interviewer some intriguing insights into what it was like to practice with the great monk.

"My teacher, Zen Master Ko Bong, came from a very high-class aristocratic family in Korea. He was very stern and correct. If he saw a crooked candle, he would straighten it. If he saw a spot of dirt, he would wipe it up. He had no temple of his own, so people would get together and invite him to come and teach them. He used to carry a long bamboo pole and walk down the middle of the meditation room. If you weren't sitting straight, if you dozed off, you got a hard whack on the part of your back between your shoulder and your lower neck. His manner was very, very hard! He never spoke of himself—ever. All of the stories about him were told by others. He was usually quite silent. If people wanted him to speak, they would give him a bottle of rice wine. He wouldn't give a Dharma talk without a drink first. Then he would give a talk—short, but very powerful. His stories were not what you would call humorous, but hard, succinct. He usually told stories from the old masters.

"Ko Bong Sunim did not drink every day. He wasn't what you would call 'dependent' on alcohol. He just liked drinking with his friends and, as I said, people would give him liquor so he would teach them, kind of to loosen his tongue. A day without drinking was a day without talking for him. Well, sometimes he would talk at special ceremonies without a drink.

"And every morning he would read the *Avatamsaka Sutra*.

"My teacher had no disciples. In those days, some Zen masters wanted lots of disciples, but my teacher had no desire for them. All he wanted was to have one keen-eyed student. Sometimes old Zen monks would visit him for Dharma combat. He would ask them a *kong-an* like, 'What is the meaning of "three pounds of flax"' People would answer with things like, 'The sky is blue; trees are green.' Well, that is right, in a way, but it did not quite make it with Ko Bong Sunim! Or other times, he would ask, 'What is the meaning of "three pounds of flax"?' and someone would give an answer right out of the *Blue Cliff Record:* '"In the north, there are pine trees; in the south, bamboo."' Same thing as the *Blue Cliff Record*!

"In these instances, Ko Bong Sunim would only shake his head, 'No good!' Many older Zen students can have a lot of pride, because they have been sitting meditation for so many years. 'Why no good? Why?!' They would get angry and leave if he did not approve of them.

"When I had an interview with Ko Bong Sunim, after I passed several other *kong-ans,* he asked me, 'The mouse eats cat food. The cat bowl is broken. What does this mean?'

"So I thought to myself, 'Cat food represents "small *I,*" OK? Mouse is "small *I.*" Then when "small *I*" is broken, true way appears. Well, this isn't that difficult. So what is the true way? The true way is "like-this": the wall is white, and the floor is brown."

"But Ko Bong Sunim said, 'No! No! No!' He only said, 'No!'

"I became very angry. Four great masters had already given me *inka,* confirming my breakthrough in practice. I had already heard some of the greatest meditation monks in the country say to me, as they gave formal approval to my insight, 'Oh, you are wonderful! You already got enlightenment, and at such a young age!' I was also very proud! So when this monk would not approve of my answer, I got very angry. I also got a big question, a great doubt. There was great anger and great doubt, two minds that fused into one: '*Yaaaahh-hhh!!* Why is my answer no good?'

"In those days, my teacher drank a lot, so sometimes he used very colorful speech. 'Nowadays practitioners are bull-shit, complete bullshit! Nobody practices hard enough any-more. Many people sit Zen, but who understands the correct way?' In the chaos of recovery from thirty-five years of Japanese occupation, the Buddhist monastic training had been severely weakened. Also, some of the senior monks had a lot of pride. Many others were attached to "monk's way"—'I am a monk, you are just a student.' There were many attachments to the lifestyle they had, attachments to sutras, and attachment to form. Most monks were proud: they had made their little 'house' inside their minds, and stayed there. You can't easily break into an old monk's house. 'I already got enlightenment,' they thought.

"This is what Ko Bong Sunim meant when he said, 'Nowadays practitioners are no good. What is happening to Korean Buddhism? Where is the correct Buddhist teaching anymore?' Whenever monks came to see him to test their insight, he saw through all of it, and only cut, cut, cut. He was very hard on everyone, and he became well known for this. And of course, he never gave *inka* to anyone. Many monks thought, 'Maybe he's just crazy!'

"But then why were all of these seasoned practitioners afraid of him? Even other Zen masters would come, and they would not dare open their mouths in front of him! If they did—*boom!*—they were totally cut down. He was absolutely ruthless. And they could not attack him, either, so even all the leading Zen masters were afraid of him, too. Then when people saw this, they would say, 'Hmmm, maybe he's not crazy after all!'

"But he never gave *inka* to anyone.

"At the time that I was having my interview with him, I did not understand anything about the world of Zen practitioners. So it was like a little dog that is unafraid of the lion. A little puppy doesn't know that a lion is strong and ferocious; he doesn't know anything! So he can yap and yap and yap and even try to attack the lion! Older dogs understand lions, so there is *no* way they would ever attempt something like that: they would just run away. But a little dog, because he doesn't know any better, will often stay to challenge the lion.

"I was like a little dog. I was still a very young monk! I did not know that this monk was so great, so strong and renowned and feared. I thought that one Zen master is just like any other Zen master. The little dog is not afraid to fight the lion, so the lion only laughs.

"So Ko Bong Sunim kept refusing my answer. 'No!' he said. And I remember thinking, 'Why no good?' There was silence for maybe fifteen minutes. Then my mind shot open, and I answered him. I remember tears running down his face—he was very happy! We call that 'Dharma happiness.' It is true happiness. You see, my teacher was very old at the time, and had no students. 'Maybe I will die soon, and not give Transmission.' He did not have a good feeling about this. And suddenly here was a young man, a boy, really, only twenty-two years old, who answers his final *kong-an*. He was able to give *inka* to one person and finish his life's work. So Ko Bong Sunim was very, very happy!"

Wild-Action Teachers

ONE DAY, a student asked Zen Master Seung Sahn, "Some Zen monks are stricter than others. And some Zen monks are more free in their style. How do we understand this?"

Dae Soen Sa Nim replied, "In Korean Buddhism, there are two kinds of Zen masters. We have sometimes heard stories about the great Zen Master Chung Soeng. He was a very free Zen master. He broke all formal style, and did many wild actions. He made many kinds of bad speech, and mouthed all sorts of foul words, and did not-so-correct actions, but this was all for teaching other people. This freedom was not for himself, for his I-my-me. Sometimes other people even had a very bad feeling about what he said or did. Later, they understood. He did not care about any action, which means that he had no I-my-me. Everything he did was reflect-action: bad action, good action doesn't matter. He did not care if somebody felt good about it or not. He only tried. This try, try, try-mind was all that mattered: no checking himself. This is one style of Zen monk.

"My grandteacher's teacher, Zen Master Kyong Ho, was

139

this style. He was a complete freedom-style monk: he did any kind of drinking and eating and action. But my grandteacher, Zen Master Man Gong, was not this style. He was always correct, correct, correct. Then my teacher, Zen Master Ko Bong, was also a freedom-style monk. As a fellow student of Man Gong Sunim, Chung Soeng Sunim is my teacher's Dharma brother, making him my Dharma uncle.

"So there are two kinds of Zen monks: Chung Soeng Sunim's freedom-style and Man Gong Sunim's correct-correct-correct style. If you are a correct-style Zen master, you have a temple and students. But if you are not so concerned with being correct, and practice and teach freedom-style, you usually have no temple and no students. If students want to have the teaching of such a teacher to get enlightenment, then they follow their freedom-style master around. So for this reason, my teacher had no real students, and neither did Chung Soeng Sunim, who could not give Transmission to anyone. He would just cut people, and they would leave.

"There are many monks who like this style. But nowadays, in some Zen centers, there are teachers who drink a lot, maybe even have sex, but still have a temple and students living with them. This is not so good. If you teach freedom-style, it is no good to keep a Zen center or temple. Why? Because students usually only follow a Zen teacher's actions, at first, when they are still young. It is like having a baby. They do not follow his teaching, or his Dharma, what he is using the freedom-actions to *point* to. Students who are just beginning their practice have no center: if they see lots of drinking and freedom-action from the very beginning, then they get some wrong idea about practicing. Then their lives are only breaking precepts and not keeping the correct Dharma rules.

"Some traditions permit this sort of behavior in the temple. A freedom-style teacher in such a tradition is often allowed to keep a temple and students, and so the students naturally see the teacher's actions every day and only follow. But this makes a problem; it is not clear at all.

"But in Korea, the situation is very clear. If you are a freedom-style Zen monk, you have no temple, and you have no students. You do not make any students, because to have students, they have to be registered first to the temple where their teacher lives and practices. The teacher must be the official leader, or connected to one, and he must live in the temple. But a freedom-style Zen monk does not have his own temple, so it turns out that he has no formal students. If one keen-eyed student appears, then he checks the student's mind, and—*boom!*—only gives *inka*. Such a monk has no regular students. This is correct Zen style.

"There is a very good story that shows this wild, freedom-style wisdom. Of course, it is a story about Zen Master Chung Soeng. One winter retreat season, a group of Zen monks asked Chung Soeng Sunim to spend the three-month intensive winter retreat with them, guiding their practice. The temple was very poor, and the monks had no money. The food was very coarse, simple fare, and they were so poor that some days they could not eat at all!

"That year was an especially cold winter. There was no wood to burn, and what is more, in those days in Korea there were very strict laws prohibiting the cutting down of trees. There had been massive deforestation during the thirty-five years of Japanese occupation and then the Korean War. So in order to promote the reforestation of Korea's denuded landscapes, the government strictly enforced adherence to this law.

Dead and fallen trees could be harvested, but nothing new could be cut down. That was a very strict rule in Korea, and is still enforced in some districts even today.

"Now, Chung Soeng Sunim was only staying for a few months. But he saw the suffering of the monks under his care, especially exposed to the brutal cold with no heat, and it pained his heart deeply. One day, he could stand it no longer. 'This temple has existed in the mountains for many centuries. Why, surrounded by trees, can the monks not be permitted to warm themselves, even just a little?' So when he heard that the housemaster was secretly permitting a few trees to come down every couple of days, he did not prevent it.

"The local chief of police, upon hearing the sound of falling trees nearby, came to the temple. 'Who is cutting down these trees?' he asked the abbot. But the abbot was reluctant to say anything, especially something that would implicate the housemaster, who was, after all, only doing his job of caring for the assembly of monks.

" 'I will ask you one more time,' the policeman said, his voice rising. 'Who cut down those trees?'

" 'I did,' one of the monks suddenly said. The next few things the monk said to the policeman were unmentionable here—they were very bad speech! All heads turned, but they already knew who it was: great Zen Master Chung Soeng!

"The policeman's face grew beet red! 'You . . . you . . . !! How dare you! Come with me!' He did not know that he was leading a great and feared Zen master away from the temple. He simply led Chung Soeng Sunim right to the nearest police station. Taking a pen and fresh paper to record any relevant information on the accused, the policeman cleared his throat officiously. 'OK, now, where are you originally from?' he asked.

"Chung Soeng Sunim's eyes brightened. 'From my father's penis!' he answered.

"'What?!' the policeman exclaimed. 'Are you crazy or something?' In those days it was especially dangerous to speak to a policeman like this, even as a joke. But Chung Soeng Sunim was not joking in the least: his face was calm and serene, and his eyes bright as crystals. This was no ordinary monk, the policeman thought. But he could tell from Chung Soeng Sunim's accent that he was not from this part of Korea, so he asked further, 'Where have you come from?'

"'From my mother's vagina!'

"'You are crazy!' the policeman shouted. 'Get out! Get out!'

"So Chung Soeng Sunim walked back to the temple. Later the police chief inquired deeper, and found out that this was a great and very honored Zen monk. So he went immediately to the temple to apologize for calling Chung Soeng Sunim 'crazy.'

"'That's OK, that's OK,' Chung Soeng Sunim said, laughing merrily. 'Crazy is no problem. Actually, crazy is good. Crazy is beautiful! Also, I was cutting down trees, so you arrested me. That is also the correct way. Ha ha ha ha!!' The police chief was very relieved, and bowed to Chung Soeng Sunim deeply three times.

"So this style of 'bad speech' and 'bad action' is also correct, since it was not 'for-me' speech. The great Zen master was using speech to teach something to the policeman. Not many people can function this way, and point to truth in this blunt yet totally honest style, but Chung Soeng Sunim could! He is pointing directly to the 'original point.' 'Where have you come from?'—the correct answer is not Boston, or Seoul, or Tokyo! Zen is a different kind of pointing. Originally, when you came into this world, where did you come from? 'From my mother's vagina!' Chung Soeng Sunim's speech is a very high-class answer, because it is true for everybody! That is what he was teaching to the policeman: everyone comes the same way. Ha ha ha ha!! This is the speech and action of a completely free man."

Intelligence in Zen?
Three Courses in Zen Math

A STUDENT AT THE New Haven Zen Center once asked Zen Master Seung Sahn, "You say that one must return to the mind of a child. Also Jesus talks like this. Then what is the role of intelligence in spirituality? What is the role of intelligence in understanding Zen?"

"What do you want, right now?" Zen Master Seung Sahn replied.

"I want peace and quiet."

"Peace? What is peace?"

"No turbulence. No movement, I guess."

"Yah, that's not bad," Zen Master Seung Sahn said. "*Peace* is a very good word. But what exactly does it mean? What is true peace?

"Sometimes we use calculators. If there is already a number on the screen, you cannot make another calculation with the calculator. The answer will not come out right. So this is why there is a button marked 'C.' If you push 'C,' the screen becomes clear: it returns to zero. Then any kind of calculation is possible.

"If you keep a clear mind, then you will get happiness everywhere. This is complete peace, like a child's mind, holding nothing whatsoever. So always just push 'C.' If your mind is angry, push 'C,' and it will become clear. If your mind is sad, push 'C,' and your mind will become clear. Don't-know mind is push-'C' mind. If you have a lot of thinking, only go straight, don't know; then your thinking will disappear.

"But when you do not return to 'zero' mind, from moment to moment, you cannot see this universe as it is. If you are thinking, then even if a mountain appears before you, you do not see this mountain; you only see your suffering thinking. If you keep a sad mind, and hold your sad mind, then even if a beautiful view appears, you cannot perceive it. You are only following your thinking. So you lose this world, from moment to moment. I always say, 'When you are thinking, you lose your eyes.' You have eyes, but when you look at something with a mind full of thinking, you do not see that thing. Also, you do not hear completely, smell completely, taste completely, or feel completely. It is like a calculator where the numbers stay stuck on the screen: you cannot do any new calculations. This is why Zen teaches that you must return to your original mind, from moment to moment. This is pushing 'C.' We call this 'only don't know.'

"When Bodhidharma first went to China, he was called in to an audience with the great Emperor Wu. This emperor was notable because he had done many, many great things to support the spread of Buddhism in his country. He had built many big temples, had sponsored the construction of many pagodas, and had disbursed vast amounts from the official treasury for the feeding and clothing of monks and the translation of sutras from India. So naturally the emperor was a little curious about how much merit he had made, and asked this distinguished guest from India, Bodhidharma.

" 'None whatsoever,' Bodhidharma replied.

"The emperor was completely shocked, because this seemed to run against what he had thought Buddhism was mainly concerned with, which he had heard was the accumulation of good merit through good works. 'If I haven't made any merit,' he asked, 'What is the highest holy truth of this Buddhist teaching?'

" 'No holiness, only vast emptiness,' Bodhidharma said.

"The emperor was flabbergasted. 'Who do you think you are? Who are you?'

" 'Don't know,' Bodhidharma replied.

"Bodhidharma was giving the emperor very high-class teaching: don't-know mind—*completely* don't-know mind—means cutting off all thinking. Your don't-know mind, my don't-know mind, Emperor Wu's don't-know mind, Bodhidharma's don't-know mind, this person's don't-know mind, Buddha's don't-know mind is the same don't-know mind.

"*Don't-know mind* means all thinking is cut off. When all thinking is cut off, mind is already empty. Empty mind is before thinking. Before thinking is your original mind. So, if you use a calculator, first you must push 'C.' Then only zero appears on the screen. This is empty mind. Empty mind is very important, because empty mind can do anything. One times zero equals zero; two times zero equals zero; one thousand times zero equals zero; mountain times zero equals zero; anger times zero equals zero; desire times zero equals zero. If your mind returns to zero, then everything is zero. Everything is empty. Completely no hindrance. Then your empty-mirror mind can reflect this universe just as it is. That is what Jesus meant when he taught, 'If you want to enter the kingdom of heaven, you must become as a child again.' A child's mind is completely empty, so it can see this world just like this. But when you hold something in your mind, you cannot reflect this world as it is, so you cannot function for others. Instead, you always get suffering.

"But this empty mind is not empty. We say it is 'empty,' but it is not empty. You can see the sky. There is daytime sky and nighttime sky. Yes, the sky is just the sky. But the daytime sky is blue; the nighttime sky is dark. Right now, the sky over us here in the United States is blue, while the sky in Korea is dark at this hour. Why is this so? After all, the sky is the same. Who made the sky blue? Who made the sky dark? What is the color of the original sky? Who *made* that color? The answer is, *you* did. The sky never said, 'I am blue.' The sky never said, 'Yah, I am dark.' You made that.

"But if you push your 'C' button—only don't know— then there is no 'blue,' no 'dark.' Everything is just-like-this. When we see sky in the day, our empty mind reflects this blueness; when seen at night, our mind reflects the darkness. That is all."

The student was silent for a few moments, then said, "I understand your speech, but I do not believe you. In fact, if you walk into a wall, it hurts. The wall is there whether you want to believe in it or not. The idealism you talk about does not work in reality."

Dae Soen Sa Nim laughed, "Yah, so when you walk into the wall, only 'Ouch!' is correct. Ha ha ha ha!! (Laughter from the audience.) You understand too much, so you are better than me! Ha ha ha ha!! I do not understand these things, but you understand a lot. You understand *too* much! So I ask you, why is the sky over America now blue, and the sky over Korea now dark? It is the same sky. Why?"

The student was silent. Then he shrugged his shoulders.

"Yah, you understand too much. And yet such a question becomes difficult to you. So we'll try this way: one plus two equals three; one plus two equals zero. Which one is correct?"

The student said, "One plus two equals three, of course."

"Correct! But 'one plus two equals zero' is also correct. You must understand this. You don't know, yah? So you must come to Zen primary school, OK? Ha ha ha ha! Every school in this world only teaches that one plus two equals three. But in the school of Zen, you first attain that one plus two equals zero. This is a very important and high-class course. It costs a lot, because it is hard on your body to come here and sit! But you must understand that one plus two equals zero.

"Before you were born, you were zero. Now you are one. In the future you will die and again become zero. So zero equals one; one equals zero. Therefore one plus two equals zero. This is Zen school. Now you understand. So I ask you, one plus two equals three; one plus two equals zero. Which one is correct? Both are correct, OK?

"But one more step is necessary. In the next course, if I ask you which one is correct and you say that both are correct, I will hit you thirty times. If you say that both are not correct, I will hit you thirty times. Then what can you do?"

The student exhaled deeply, "Ah, I—" His hands flopped limply in his lap. "Hnnnggg . . ."

Dae Soen Sa Nim leaned forward toward him, his eyes glinting. "OK, I ask you: is zero a number?"

"Not exactly," the man said. "Well, yes and no, I suppose."

"If you say it is a number, it's a number. If you say it's not a number, it's not a number."

"Not exactly," the student said quickly.

"If you say 'not exactly,' I will hit you. If you say that it is a number, I will hit you. If you say that it is not a number, I will also hit you. This is the second course, because if you completely *attain* zero—which means, if you completely attain the *nature* of zero—then there is no Buddha, no God, no mind, no I, no you, no name, no form, nothing at all. And so in true zero, if you open your mouth to express that or any of this, you are also wrong. This is the second course.

"So only *do* it—only don't know. This don't-know mind is already before thinking. Before thinking there is no speech, no words. So opening your mouth to express anything about it is already a big mistake. Don't-know mind is your primary point. Maybe someone says that this primary point is 'mind,' or 'Buddha,' or 'God,' or 'consciousness,' or 'the Absolute,' or 'energy,' or 'substance,' or 'nature,' or 'everything.' But the true primary point has no name and no form. There are no speech or words for it. If you keep a don't-know mind, you are already before thinking. Before thinking is your substance, and this substance has no name and no form. Then what can you do?

"When someone asked the great Zen Master Lin Chi, 'What is Buddha?' he only shouted, 'KATZ!'* When someone would ask such questions of Zen Master Dok Sahn, he would only hit the questioner with his stick—*boom!* And when someone would ask Zen Master Guji, he would simply raise one

---

*KATZ! (sometimes transliterated as "HAL!"): a sudden shout originating deep in the lower abdomen, or "center." This is used as a wordless experession that cuts off all conceptual, discriminative thinking, delivering the listener to a direct experience of nonduality.

finger. These Zen masters did not open their mouths. They did not use words or speech: only a wordless transmission from me to you.

"But many people think that this transmission from mind to mind is something difficult or mysterious. It is not.

"I often express it like this: when I first began living in the United States, I started noticing how a certain truck would drive slowly past the Zen center every afternoon, playing strange music. I did not understand what was going on. It happened at about the same time every day, while I was sitting in meditation, so I could not see anything out the window. And every single day this music was the same. Not very high-class music! Then one day I decided to look out the window, and saw many children running toward the truck. 'Yahhhh! Ice cream!' they were shouting.

"So I understood. The ice cream man did not open his mouth. He only played music. Then everyone understood: ice cream. The ice cream man was using music to transmit ice-cream mind to the children's mind, who already understood it. This is a kind of wordless transmission.

"First, there is talking about emptiness, about zero mind: 'Zero equals one, one equals zero.' Next, if you do not stop there, and completely attain zero, there is no talking. Only hit, only 'KATZ!,' only lifting one finger, and then you already understand. One day the Buddha was ready to give a Dharma speech. More than one thousand disciples gathered, waiting for his speech. 'How will he teach us about truth today?' they wondered. 'What kind of teaching?' But the Buddha did not open his mouth. One minute passed. Two minutes. Five minutes. Ten minutes. 'What is wrong? Maybe he is sick today?' they thought. Then he reached down and plucked a flower, lifting it over his head wordlessly. The disciples all stared at him in befuddled wonderment. Only one disciple, Mahakashyapa, seated far in the rear of the assembly, smiled broadly, 'Waahhhhh!' Seeing this, the Buddha said, 'I transmit my true Dharma to you alone.' When the Buddha picked up a flower and Mahakashyapa saw that, he smiled: the dialogue was already finished. This is Zen.

"So if you attain zero, then your mind is already empty mind. *Empty mind* means that your mind is clear like empty space. *Clear like space* means that it is clear like a mirror: it reflects everything. When a red ball comes before the mirror, a red ball appears; when a white ball comes, a white ball appears. Someone is sad, I am sad. Someone is happy, then I am happy. This is the bodhisattva: no desire for myself, my actions are only for all beings. This is Great Love and the Great Bodhisattva Way. This is world peace and your true peace. You originally said that you want 'peace,' so I am pointing to what true peace is. Every religion and people has their different idea of peace: Christian peace, American peace, Chinese peace, French peace. It is all different, because it is all based entirely on thinking. So they are fighting over their idea of peace. That is not true peace!

"So, if you want true and correct peace, you must come to the Zen center and attain that one plus two equals zero. Then you must completely attain this zero, and then attain that the truth is just-like-this. The sky is blue, and trees are green. Your mind is an empty mirror, and perceives this world just as it is. Then from here you can function compassionately only to help all beings. This is a kind of Zen course: primary school, high school, university! Ha ha ha ha!"

The student laughed, too, and bowed. "Thank you for your teaching."

Homesick

ONE DAY, a bookish young student of Zen Master Seung Sahn was sitting at the Providence Zen Center, diligently devouring a text, when suddenly, he felt someone patting him lightly on the shoulder. Startled, he looked back to see that the Zen master had come up quietly behind him.

"You're homesick, very homesick . . ." the Zen master said, continuing to pat him gently, his round face filled with soft compassion.

But this speech startled the student more than his teacher's sudden appearance. "I do not miss my home, or my family," he thought to himself. "How could he think I am homesick for those things?"

Just as he thought this, the Zen master continued, ". . . homesick for your *original* home."

Shocked at such recognition of the sadness in his mind, the student bowed quietly.

Learning from Las Vegas

ZEN MASTER SEUNG SAHN and several of his students were transporting a Buddha statue from the Providence Zen Center to a temple in Los Angeles. It was the early 1970s, and one of his American students suggested he see the country. So the Zen master and three or four others piled into an old Volkswagen van and wheeled their way onto the vast, open road, all of them taking turns at the wheel.

After several days of travel, they were finally nearing California. The glimmering lights of Las Vegas beckoned from afar as they crossed the desert floor. Since it was already past midnight, they decided to park for the night in the city. There would be many faithful greeting them on their arrival in Los Angeles the next day, and long ceremonies at the temple. So the American students immediately took the opportunity to grab some sleep, and slumped in their seats where they sat.

But their lone Korean passenger had never seen Las Vegas before. Bathed in the Vegas Strip's fantastic blinking lights, he was too curious and excited to sleep. So he told them he was going out for a walk, and left.

Some time later, the snoozing students were aroused by a sudden, van-heaving *boom!* The back door was flung wide open and there was Zen Master Seung Sahn, standing with legs akimbo, one hand on his hip and the other furiously waving them out. "Wake up! Everybody wake up!"

"Whuhhh! Hey, it's almost four o'clock." "Wha's happening?!" the startled students stammered, rubbing their eyes.

"Everybody come out now! We go over there!" Reaching in, Dae Soen Sa Nim began pulling people out, moving to the side doors to have better access to the bodies slumped in the center seats. "Come on! Come on!"

He marched the sleepy gaggle of students through the center doors of one of the largest casinos on the Las Vegas Strip. It was still the middle of the night, yet the vast, red-carpeted floor was still chock-full of people. The doormen looked askance at this crew of mangy hippies and their bald, gray-suited, electric leader, his arm outstretched and gesturing far to the back of the casino, grabbing his students' arms as he emphasized its vastness.

As far back as they could see, it was an ocean of machines, furiously blinking lights, and bleeping sounds emerging from layers of a thickly cigaretted haze. The slot machines in particular were well attended. Waitresses in pink miniskirts ferried an endless supply of food, drinks, and buckets of quarters to the gamers, their tired frames partly slumped against their machines.

A multitude of arms rose and yanked down the slot-machine levers with mechanical rhythm. Wiping their tired eyes, holding cigarettes with unattended ashes drooping down, they seemed fleshly connections of this vast electric apparatus, into which they seemed to dump an endless stream of quarters, fearing that to let go of the machine would be to offer up the accumulation of good luck and a just-around-the-corner jackpot to the next gamer. Occasionally there was a drunken rant. Someone would be led away. Or a tense argument would break out over too much loud praying for the next jackpot.

So they stayed. The American Zen students stood there, taking it all in. It was an unreal reality not dreamed of in their Zen philosophy. Finally one of them, snapping to, noticed that the Zen master had disappeared.

"Oh, my God! Where is Dae Soen Sa Nim?"

Suddenly, Zen Master Seung Sahn strode out of the smoky haze. He carried two sacks in his hands, and the weight pulled his shoulders down slightly. Reaching his students, he grabbed fistfuls of rolled quarters from the bags and began distributing them to the students. Now everyone was thoroughly confused!

"Go play! Go play! Go play!" he shouted, waving them out into the floor.

The students in their hippie beads and floral peace shirts were incredulous. "But Zen Master, how can we do this?" one of them asked. Zen students in those days were especially proud of their countercultural stance, rejecting particularly such garish displays of conspicuous consumption as this.

Another chimed in, "Yeah, isn't this against the tenets of Zen, to gamble and waste money like this?"

Dae Soen Sa Nim's face suddenly grew serious. "Do you see those people?" He pointed out in a grand sweeping gesture to the hazy, blinking casino floor that spread out before them. "These people are all trapped in hell—the hell of their own desires. All of you are practicing the Great Bodhisattva Way, which means always having a mind that does together-action with all beings. If you do not understand their kind of hell, how will you ever save them?"

And with that, he reached back into the bag for more bunches of rolled quarters. This time, his students gladly accepted them.

A Good Sense of Direction

ONE DAY, a student said to Zen Master Seung Sahn, "I have a problem with directions. Anywhere I go, I always get lost. I cannot drive anywhere without asking directions, and even then it doesn't work! It is very frustrating because my boyfriend is always making jokes about this, and I have to laugh, but inside I am suffering. How can I change this?"

Dae Soen Sa Nim replied, "OK, this problem is very simple, not complicated. First you must understand what is correct direction. Any time that you are thinking, you cannot find the right direction. You cannot tell what is north, south, east, or west. That is because if you are thinking, and attached to this thinking, then even though you feel the correct way, inside, you are always checking yourself. 'Maybe it wasn't this way. Maybe I should try some other way.' This kind of mind. Even if you look at a very high-class map, yet hold your thinking, and check your mind, you cannot find the true way. So that is very interesting!

"Actually everyone already understands which way they should go, at every moment. It is not something that you

157

learn; it is something that you already know. Another word for this is *intuition*.

"Look at the animal world for a moment: every kind of animal must constantly move, back and forth, here and there, many times every single day. Animal life is very simple: if an animal does not move, it cannot find food, or else maybe some other animal uses *it* for food! Ha ha ha ha! Then it will die. So animals are constantly on the move, and their lives depend on how well they move. Sometimes they must travel in the dark, or fly many thousands of miles to find their homes. You have heard of salmon traveling many hundreds of miles to find the place where they were born, even swimming up against the tide to get there. They never doubt their direction.

"When human beings look at this situation, they think, 'Waahhh!! That is a very *mysterious* ability. Animals are very stupid things: how come they can do that?' But if you look closely at animals, you can see why. They have no thinking. Animals have very simple minds: when they see something, they *just* see—no thinking. When they hear something, they *just* hear—no thinking. When they smell something, they *just* smell—no thinking. When they taste, or feel something across their skin—maybe the wind, or a vibration—they *just* feel it, with no thinking. It is very easy!

"That means that animals can completely become one with their environment, and what it is saying to them. And since they completely believe their eyes, ears, nose, tongue, body, and mind, when they perceive something, there is no separation whatsoever: they can just *do* it. To an animal, there is no yesterday or tomorrow—there is only this moment.

"But human beings have too much thinking. Actually, human beings can do the same things as animals. Yet human beings' thinking grew up too quickly, and became too strong: it is not balanced with the rest of their lives. And so human beings depend on thinking too much to survive in this world. Thinking *itself* is not good, not bad. But if you attach to something—even a good thing—you have a problem.

"Instead of believing their eyes, ears, nose, tongue, body, and mind, human beings only believe their thinking, and then hold their thinking, and check their thinking. This is very bad. That is why you can see that some human beings who study too many books or use their heads too much often cannot find their way around outside. But people who keep a very pure and clear mind—like a farmer, or someone who is not complicated—have a very good sense of direction. They just hear some directions one time, and—*boom!*—it makes an image in their heads. Or they understand the angle of the sun as they move, or the wind, and decide according to this. Then when they are driving or walking, they can find this place very easily. Farmers smell rain or snow the day before it comes. Their thinking and seeing and hearing and smelling and taste and touch all become one: there is no 'inside,' there is no 'outside.' Everything completely becomes one.

"So, if you want to find your correct direction, you must watch an animal. Do you have a dog? A cat?"

"I have a dog," the student replied.

"Good! That dog must become your teacher! Ha ha ha ha!! Just watch this dog, then soon you will understand. Yah, some dogs have different karma, which means different thinking. You know how we say that one dog is very smart, while another is very stupid? This stupid dog cannot find things well, or sometimes takes a long time to find his way home. That is because dogs and some animals have a very little thinking, or karma. They can also have some kind of emotional karma. So this becomes a hindrance. Maybe this comes from living with human beings too much. Ha ha ha!!

"But if you look at dogs, there is no hindrance in their eyes or ears or nose or tongue. So they can do many, many interesting things. They can even lead blind human beings around.

"So, if you want to have a good sense of direction, you must let go of your thinking—only go straight, don't know. Then you can believe your eyes, ears, nose, tongue, body, and mind. You can believe this world. This is how you find your right way home, OK?"

The student bowed.

Great Suffering, Great Vow

THERE ARE MANY, many examples of the power of Zen Master Seung Sahn's Great Vow. His every gesture, every inflection of speech, the intensity of his eyes—and also their softness—revealed it. I have played some tapes of his Dharma talks in Korean to people who don't understand Korean, and they can feel the intensity, the dedication, the effort, the one-pointedness, but especially the compassion, in his voice. And Koreans who listen to his English-language tapes can feel it just as well.

But in any language, the master always conveys the power of the Great Vow. There is a story that expresses this well: one very respectable Korean doctor I know spent many, many sleepless nights continually harassed by horrible demons. The demons were totally real to her—she could even smell them, and they beat her and several times even raped her. She had physical injuries from them. I tried giving her all kinds of advice about how to practice, but none of it helped her. She was completely miserable.

Then one day, I gave her a set of Zen Master Seung Sahn's

talks in Korean on the Mu Mun Kwan ("The Gateless Gate," a collection of forty-eight traditional *kong-ans*). Recorded on cassette some seventeen years ago, they are recordings of Zen Master Seung Sahn lecturing in an animated, humorous, very intense voice. I have always thought, when listening to these, that if one could record the sound of the Great Vow, this is what it would sound like. I know this doctor well enough to know that she wouldn't have the time or the energy, at the end of a long day, to take pains to listen to *what* was being said. And I know that she would have absolutely no interest in *kong-ans*. But I hoped that if she could just hear the sound of his voice as she lay in bed . . .

The doctor looked at me a little curiously when I handed it to her. "Is this Buddhist chanting?" she asked.

"No," I said. "Just my teacher, giving some talks."

"But is there any music with it? How am I supposed to listen to lectures in bed? Now I'm really not going to be able to sleep."

The next day I got a call from her. "You'll never believe it! I had my first full night of sleep in weeks! No demons appeared! No demons appeared!" She was very happy, and for the first time in many months her voice sounded not so ragged with anxiety. "I played your teacher's tapes, and his voice was so clear, so strong! I don't really understand what he's talking about, but just the sound of his voice made my mind so relaxed and clear!"

Since that day, the "demons" have never appeared again. She needed the tapes for a week or two after that, but from that point on, she could sleep without them. It seems that the sound of Zen Master Seung Sahn's voice had chased all of her demons away!

Invariably, nearly any individual or group, when presented with a photo of Zen Master Seung Sahn or a recording of the sound of his speech, has always been able to feel in some way the force of his unshakeable direction, his devotion to the Way and to saving all beings. And we can all feel very strongly that this person has been pursuing this for many, many lifetimes: we call this the *Great Vow*.

Of course, we have all heard stories about Zen Master Seung Sahn's Great Vow: in fact, I doubt there is any story about him that is *not* in some way a story about the Great Vow, or a manifestation of it.

But of the many, many examples of his Great Vow that I saw with my own eyes and ears, one in particular stands out. It made such a strong, abiding impression on me because, at the time, Zen Master Seung Sahn was physically suffering quite badly: many of us believed that he was at death's door, and that we could not expect that he would ever be able to go back to Hwa Gye Sah Temple, his temple in the mountains outside Seoul. Some people were talking very seriously, in low tones, about funeral plans should his health take a turn for the worse, which was widely expected.

Zen Master Seung Sahn was hospitalized in Seoul for several months in late winter and early spring of 2003. Though his body was in great physical pain, he would not allow himself to be confined to his bed. He insisted, every minute or two, to make a circuit around the floor where he was housed. Although he could walk, we drove him around in a wheelchair to protect him from losing too much energy. He insisted on these circuits around the hospital without fail, even doing them throughout the long and painful nights when sleep itself was not possible. Many of his students had the honor of pushing his chair around, and the route that was to be followed was exactly the same, every time. Should a new person unfamiliar with this ritual fail to take the correct route—straight down the hall, turn right along the atrium windows, then straight again, making a left at the elevators, crossing over to the other side of the elevator banks, making a sharp left, heading straight down to the nurses' station, hooking another sharp left, and completing the long straightaway back to his room on the right—Zen Master Seung Sahn never failed to correct them. We realized after a time that he insisted on this circuit being repeated exactly the same way, over and over and over again, in order to test his own mind, and keep himself sharp in the midst of this long and tedious hospitalization.

On one of these circuits, I was accompanying him together with Zen Master Dae Kwan, a great nun and abbot of the Su Bong Zen Monastery in Hong Kong. Zen Master Seung Sahn must have been having a particularly difficult day, because as we escorted him away from the room, he began to say out loud, to no one in particular, in his "Much pain! Much pain! My body have much pain!"

Hearing this, Dae Kwan Sunim leaned over and said to him, "Sir, please give your pain to us. We want to take your pain." It wasn't a Dharma combat challenge; the sadness and concern on Dae Kwan Sunim's face were clearly evident. It was just a simple gesture of a student's compassion for her teacher.

"What say?" Dae Soen Sa Nim asked, cocking his head in her direction, then in mine.

"I said, Please give your pain to us: 50 percent to me, 50 percent to Hyon Gak Sunim! Please give us your pain, sir!"

But Dae Soen Sa Nim only waved his hand over his lap in dismissive refusal. "No, no, no, no! It's enough only I experience this. Never give to you—only I keep!"

But Dae Kwan Sunim was not going to give up so easily. "No, sir. We want to take your pain away!"

"You cannot," Dae Soen Sa Nim replied. "My pain is very expensive!"

"How much, sir?" I asked him. "We will buy it from you."

"My pain is so expensive, you cannot buy it!"

Dae Kwan Sunim leaned into his ear and said, "Then maybe I will sell the Su Bong Zen Monastery, and get lots of money, and give it to you. Then you give us your pain!"

At these words, Zen Master Seung Sahn only kept silence. But it wasn't a lack of answer: when a tiger crouches low, ready to strike, though it may be silent and completely motionless, only a fool would describe this as inactivity. So Dae Soen Sa Nim remained silent as the wheelchair continued moving several more feet across the cleanly carpeted hospital floor.

"If we give you all of this money, then what will you do with it?" Dae Kwan Sunim finally asked him.

"I take your money, then rent another Zen center, save all beings from suffering! Ha ha ha ha!" At these words, we all burst out laughing. Then he just as suddenly said, "That's not a bad business deal, yah?"

We laughed and laughed and laughed. But more than just humor, I remember laughing out of pure relief. I remember thinking, "Waah! The Great Tiger has not forgotten his job!!" That same night, back at the temple, as I lay in bed waiting for sleep, remembering this best Dharma talk I had ever heard, given by the old master from his wheelchair, tears welled up in my eyes.

Women Cannot Get Enlightenment!

ONE DAY, ONE OF ZEN MASTER SEUNG SAHN'S female American students asked him, "Sir, are there any women Zen masters in Korea?"

"No, no, no!" he quickly replied. "Of course not!"

The student was completely shocked, even angered by this, more so because Zen Master Seung Sahn himself had always treated his female students with complete equality, and even formally authorized several of them to teach. "How could he think like this?" she thought. "This is completely outrageous." After a few moments, she stammered out, "But how is this possible?"

Eyeing her and half-smiling, he replied, "Because women cannot get enlightenment!"

This was unbelievable! Half-expecting that he was joking, she looked up, but by then he had already marched into another room. She followed him, where he had busied himself with some things, almost as if the conversation had never occurred.

"I have been practicing with you for several years now,"

she continued. "You have always just taught us to believe in our true self 100 percent. How can you possibly now say that women cannot get enlightenment?"

Wheeling around sharply, Zen Master Seung Sahn pointed his finger at her and, looking into her eyes strongly, said, "So, you're a 'woman'?"

The student was silent as his teaching sank in.

Letter to a Dictator

EDITOR'S NOTE

PRESIDENT PARK CHUNG-HEE was assassinated by his appointed director of South Korea's Central Intelligence Agency on October 26, 1979, ending twenty-eight years of rule. A brief interregnum was followed, on December 12, by the beginning of a coup d'état, led by a group of military officers under the leadership of General Chun Du-Hwan. Under the banner of extreme anticommunism the general led a brutal crackdown on perceived foes of the government, particularly those favoring democratization and an end to military dictatorship. As part of ongoing protests against General Chun Du-Hwan's rule, thousands of students and ordinary citizens in the southern provincial capital of Kwangju took to the streets in May 1980. They eventually overran police stations, and brought the city to a virtual standstill in a mass demonstration.

In events that many believe could not have happened without the tacit agreement and, perhaps, collusion of American military authorities then controlling South Korean security services, one of the darkest chapters in Korea's history then began to unfold: on May 18, the central government severed all phone, communication, and travel links to Kwangju, cutting it off from the outside world. Thousands of Korean special forces paratroopers began dropping into the city. A large-scale massacre of the citizens of Kwangju began. Official estimates of close to two hundred citizens killed and three thousand injured are disputed by scholars, who estimate the deaths and missing at four or five times the official amount.

The country was plunged into further chaos, and thousands of students and workers were arrested and brutally tortured. Ordinary people who were even suspected of opposition to the regime—in thought, word, or deed—were routinely rounded up: the lucky ones were tortured and released. Those less fortunate were simply never heard from again. The wounds of President Chun's extreme right-wing rule are still visible in the South Korea of today.

It was against this backdrop that one day in 1982, Zen Master Seung Sahn picked up a pen and wrote the following letter to President Chun.

The extreme danger in which he placed himself through this action cannot be overstated. Since he continually traveled back and forth to Korea, he could have been imprisoned and tortured, or worse, killed. Such occurrences were not uncommon, and his status as a monk did not exempt him from what others faced. Contemporary Koreans who have read this letter routinely exclaim shock and disbelief. This is especially true when the letter is read in its original Korean: Dae Soen Sa Nim sharply criticizes and even mocks the president, albeit in polite terms.

The ancient histories of China, Korea, and Japan are frequently peopled with great monks who rose to the position of Royal Preceptor, or National Teacher. From this position, they were empowered to educate the throne and the court—and help guide the nation. This letter stands firmly in an Asian tradition stretching back into antiquity: a mountain sage fearlessly transmitting enlightened guidance to a ruler trapped in the briars of unbridled power. More than just a cautioning against abuse of power, it is a call for the ruler to become a true leader. And to find that, the leader must first understand himself: "How can you rule a country of millions correctly when you do not even know who you are?" Political science, according to Zen.

The letter was written in Zen Master Seung Sahn's distinctive longhand, on clean typing paper, and mailed directly to President Chun. Zen Master Seung Sahn instructed his American secretary to translate the letter immediately into English. It was never distributed, either in Korean or in English, or revealed publicly. Only a few of his closest students had ever seen it, or knew of its existence, until now.

The letter was mailed in late August or early September of 1982. The next time Zen Master Seung Sahn traveled to South Korea, with a group of his Western students, he was met at the airport by black-suited security agents wearing dark sunglasses. They separated him from his American students, who looked on in shock as their teacher was taken to a black car, parked at the curb. One of the students remembers that, though the normally smiling and ebullient Zen master momentarily blinked a worried look, in a second he returned to mirrorlike form, and reassured his students in his chopped English as he was whisked away, "Don't worry. No problem. Only go to Hwa Gye Sah Temple. I soon coming." He was placed in a car.

He was driven away to the headquarters of the Korean

Central Intelligence Agency (KCIA), deep under Nam Sahn Mountain, in central Seoul. He was interrogated for several hours, as dark-suited functionaries of the nervous security apparatus and even the president's own security detail probed the Zen master to learn of his ulterior political motives for writing the letter. Finding nothing, he was released that same day.

Upon returning to Hwa Gye Sah Temple, he related to his students that, when the door was first opened for him and he was placed in the car at the airport, there was only one person in the back seat: a prominent official from the KCIA. As Zen Master Seung Sahn said to his students about the meeting: "There was no speech between us. He looked into my face for a long time, not saying anything, trying to see something about me, maybe my intentions. He just checked my eyes. Also I checked his eyes. Two old tigers facing each other, checking each other's eyes. Ha ha ha!!"

President Chun Du-Hwan stepped down in 1988. Charged with crimes of abuse of power and corruption, and hounded by students demonstrating against his alleged abuses, particularly the Kwangju massacre, he and his wife (both devout Christians at the time) chose internal exile and repentance at Baek Dahm Sah Temple, one of the most deeply remote temples in South Korea, located far in the snowbound recesses of Sorak Sahn Mountain. He remained there for many months.

In 1994, one of Zen Master Seung Sahn's monastic students suggested a meeting with the former dictator at Baek Dahm Sah Temple. Though exiled and disgraced, hated by many and rejected by his Christian churchmen, the aging dictator still wielded great power. Perhaps, it was suggested, the Zen master could guide him to deeper self-reflection and repentance? So along with one of his American monastic students, Zen Master Seung Sahn traveled to Baek Dahm Sah for the meeting.

They had lunch in the cafeteria, the former general and president now dressed in humble gray temple clothes. From time to time, someone of the resident monks would stop at their table to ask if the food was satisfactory, bowing deeply and officiously greeting the former dictator with the high honorific titles and word choice reserved exclusively, in South Korea, for the president. Dae Soen Sa Nim, his attendant recalled, addressed his tablemate with the everyday politeness and style used for any normal layman. The barrel-chested, military man drew his chin back and in, bolt upright at this smiling monk's obvious fearlessness. After lunch, when they sat down for tea, Zen Master Seung Sahn asked the president if he remembered any of what was written in "the letter."

"What letter? What are you talking about?"

Zen Master Seung Sahn motioned to his American student. The young monk reached in his bag and pulled out a long envelope bearing the seal of the Providence Zen Center. He offered this envelope to the president, whose face was now narrowed into a tight scowl. Zen Master Seung Sahn watched as the former dictator opened the envelope and began to read. President Chun's face grew red with rage as he went through the letter, his eyes darting back and forth sharply as they greedily devoured every line. His breathing became noticeably more apparent. The tension in the room was thick, as his attendants warily eyed each other, fully expecting the imminent blowup of President Chun's famous temper.

Draining his cup of tea, Zen Master Seung Sahn smiled broadly, satisfied to see that the teaching was finally reaching its target. He motioned to his attendants, and they left.

What follows is the letter the dictator read.

LETTER TO A DICTATOR

Providence Zen Center
Cumberland, R.I.
August 25, 1982

Dear President Chun,
Greeting you in the name of the Three Jewels—Buddha, Dharma, and Sangha.

Time flies swiftly as an arrow, and it is already more than two years since you became President of Korea. During that time, you have been working hard in the name of our country and our people. I send my concern that this has not been too hard on your health.

I am not writing in order to discuss whether or not your rule has been "good" or "bad." Nowadays in society we see so much fighting and quarreling over "right" and "wrong." In the world of human beings, this is an old and endless struggle. But if, instead of engaging in this sort of fighting, we were to ask ourselves, "What is the nature of 'good'?" and "What is the nature of 'evil'?" "What is the nature of this universe?" or "What is the nature of 'time' and 'space,' and do they really exist at all?" such petty arguing would immediately disappear and we would instantly begin to see the world of truth.

An eminent teacher once said,

Good and evil have no self-nature.
"Enlightened" and "unenlightened" are empty names.

174

In front of the doors* is a land of perfect stillness and
    light:
Spring comes, and grass grows by itself.

So, "good" and "evil" do not possess any self-existent nature. It is merely our *thinking* that makes "good" or "evil."
Then, if we cut off all thinking, where is the existence of good
and bad, life and death, or upper-class and lower-class? If we
find our original human face, which is present before thinking
arises, we will be able to transform this world into a realm of
freedom and equality.

This is why I do not wish to discuss here whether your
rule has been just or unjust. Rather, I am writing this letter
because tears well up in my eyes when I see our beloved country divided in two, and the needless suffering that this causes.

Sir, while still in middle school, I spent four months in jail
as a political prisoner during the Japanese occupation of
Korea. After our liberation from Japanese rule, I participated
in the student movements that actively opposed Kim Il-Sung
in North Korea, and was forced to flee south. Then while I
was in college, I witnessed pro-Western and pro-communist
students massing separately in different parts of Seoul to mark
the March 1, 1919, national holiday celebrating our common
uprising against Japanese colonial rule. Both groups eventually
marched into the plaza in front of Seoul's central train station,
where I saw them fighting and even shooting at and killing
each other. I cannot tell you how sick and heartbroken it made
me to see this! In that moment, I said to myself, "Ahhh, this

---

*In Buddhist teaching, the ports or "doors" through which we engage the sensory
world of experience: the eyes, ears, nose, tongue, body, and mind.

is truly the end of Korea! How can we kill each other on such a sacred day?"

I could no longer endure this situation, so I entered the deep mountains, cut my hair, and became a monk. It has now been nearly forty years since I made that decision.

As you know, after liberation from Japan, there was a song popular among children whose words were, "Do not be deceived by the Russians; / Don't depend on the Americans; / And Japan will rise again." These words have now become the reality.

Sir, we Koreans are a people of wisdom who respect ethics, are very devoted to classical Oriental traditions, with refined aesthetics and scholarship. We are a great and proud people. Since first coming to the United States some thirteen years ago, I have worked hard to show many Western people how to find their true self through Zen practice. While traveling throughout the United States and the world, I have expressed the great pride I have in our people, and have explained on many occasions how even our national flag is based on the principles of Eastern philosophy. I have used this to show what a philosophical and wide-minded people we truly are.

It is not my wish to make this a long story, but I cannot help but point you to one thing: in our mind, there is no north or south, no life or death, no time or space. We are already perfectly complete.

But when thinking appears, mind appears. And when mind appears, all sorts of opinions appear, egoistic attachment appears, I-my-me. This is the reason for making "right-wing" and "left-wing," and judging them to be either "good" or "bad." Attachment to thinking is the cause of all this arguing and fighting over "good" and "bad." This is the cause of our attachment to life and death. Who could expect world peace to appear through such conditions?

The possibility of reunifiying North and South Korea is intimately linked with the possibility of world peace. Yet how can we ever expect world peace when politicians, scholars, and religious leaders all claim that they and those who think like them are right, while others who do not think just like them are all wrong?

However, I beg you to imagine a world wherein anyone who aspires to be a politician, scholar, or religious teacher first makes effort to discover his true self, and only then performs the role of politician, scholar, or religious teacher. World peace would spring out instantaneously! This is the goal to which I devote all of my meager efforts.

Thus I urge you, as president of our country, to lead a nationwide campaign to find our original human nature, our true self. When many people accomplish this work, quarreling will cease, and not only will we attain an absolute world in which "right" and "wrong," and "good" and "evil" no longer exist, but your presidency could be said to have had some value, despite the many sufferings it has brought.

I am compelled to write to you with such urgency because great difficulties for every individual, every nation, and every people will intensify from now until Sakura flowers bloom in the spring of 1984. Unless you attain your true self, you will face even greater personal sufferings, too.

So, it is important to keep this in mind, as an eminent teacher once said:

> All formations are impermanent.
> This is the law of appearing and disappearing.

When both appearing and disappearing disappear,
Then this stillness is bliss.

Everything in this world is always changing, changing, changing, changing: that is the law of appearing and disappearing. But when mind disappears, our opinions and our attachment to I-my-me disappear. When we experience this state of perfect selflessness, or "no I," then everything that we see and hear is the truth. The sky is blue: that is truth. Trees are green: that is truth. Water is flowing: that is truth. A dog barks, "Woof! Woof!" Birds are singing, "Cheep, cheep, cheep!" Salt is salty, and sugar is sweet: this is the absolute truth. Right now we are all living in a world of truth. But because human beings do not know their true nature, they do not see and hear and smell the truth-world in which they live.

Sir, I am not interested in discussing your performance in office. Whether you are right or wrong in your policies or actions, you are still the president of the country. As president, you have a duty to lead and govern the Korean people well. Whatever may have been the past actions of your administration, that is all past and done. Rather, you should ask yourself now how you can improve the real lives of your countrymen.

I know that there are those who wish to foment religious conflict and misunderstanding in Korea. How can we say that this is correct? Certain religious leaders constantly talk about whether or not people are following the "right" religion, or whether or not the people believe in *their* particular faith, which they take to be the only correct one. But a true person of religion, whether other people like his religion or not, must use love and compassion to lead all sentient beings to the world of truth, to paradise. All religions have the same purpose; only the methods employed to achieve that purpose are different.

You will have a much easier job of governing the country if you are able to cause people of different religions—particularly, religious leaders—to attain their true nature, and thereby attain absolute truth, before they take on the responsibilities of political or spiritual leadership.

An eminent teacher once wrote,

> Heaven is earth, earth is heaven: heaven and earth
> revolve.
> Water is mountain, mountain is water: water and
> mountain are empty.
> Heaven is heaven, earth is earth: when did they ever
> revolve?
> Mountain is mountain, water is water: each is separate
> from the other.

This poem points directly to the human nature and universal substance that I am talking about. Human beings are very foolish, because while they claim to know many, many things, they do not have the faintest idea who they themselves really are!

So, if you attain your own self-nature, "north" and "south" will disappear from your mind, and the reunification of Korea will happen much sooner than you think. If all Koreans simply turned their attention to attaining their true mind, then the way to reunification would be an easy one.

> The Great Way has no gate;
> The tongue has no bone.

Spring sunlight fills everywhere.
Willow is green, and flowers are red.

We Koreans are pure-minded, sophisticated, and philosophical people. But throughout our history, and especially
since liberation from Japanese rule, politicians have killed the
Korean people's spirit and are encouraging them to behave
like fighting animals.

Sir, let us look at the problem from another way: two or
three thousand years ago, the earth's population was around
500–700 million people. In those days, people lived more hap-
pily together, helping and loving one another while living in
harmony with their environment. But now, in 1982, the population of the world has passed the five-billion-humans mark.
Where do you think these people came from? Do you think
God made them? Or did Buddha make them? I will give you
a hint: in this world, cause and effect are already very clear.
Nothing happens by pure accident. That you became president is your karma, and it is part of Korea's karma as well.

So, we know that, since time immemorial, human beings
have killed animals and have enjoyed eating their flesh. The
result of this is that people have unknowingly eaten their own
flesh. According to Judeo-Christian teachings, God gave
human beings dominion over the earth, and with it, the right
to kill and eat all of the animals they wished. This sort of
teaching encouraged a machinelike, materialism-oriented society such as we find dominating Western civilization, which
inspired the appearance then of communism: both of these
teachings privileged a kind of mindless, competitive, dog-eat-
dog lifestyle over and above any value for insight into true

human nature. The countries of the West, as I write this, are seeking to defend their way of life through the stockpiling of nuclear arms. But who can guarantee that someone one day will not use these weapons to destroy the whole human race?

Meanwhile, animals must be reborn. Due to other karmic factors operating alongside the conditions of their death, many of them can take form as human beings. They may appear in this world as human beings, carrying with them a mind of "balancing" their deaths, a kind of revenge. That is why we can see ever-increasing cases of youngsters who not only do not heed their parents' words, but even kill their parents with axes or knives. That is why a young policeman went berserk recently here in the West and killed many, many people. That is why mass disasters such as airplane and other transportation accidents occur so often. That is why the Argentine government recently started a needless war against mighty Great Britain that resulted in the pointless deaths of many people. And that is why Korea has allowed itself to be deceived by Russia and America for thirty-seven years since the end of World War II, and cannot even be called a truly independent nation anymore.

Because human beings have come to crave the taste of meat, many animals have potentially been reborn in human form to revenge or "balance" their deaths. This is only the law of cause and effect! So it is not an accident that people so often use phrases such as "son of a bitch," "jackass," "monkey," "bird brain," and "dirty rat" to describe or curse other people. That is because many humans still have this dog-mind, or donkey-mind, or cow-mind, or monkey-mind, or snake-mind functioning inside them still, from past lives, that these qualities so easily appear to others.

Shakyamuni Buddha taught us not to kill any living being. He taught us that every sentient being has an absolute right to live.

We Koreans use the term "dog party" a lot. This refers to a situation of total chaos and confusion, where everything is out of harmony. Do you recall the events resulting in your ascension to the presidency of Korea? After the former president, Park Chung-Hee, was assassinated, the "three Kims" dominating Korean political life—Kim Dae-Jung, Kim Jong-Pil, and Kim Yong-Sam—all had their eyes fixed on a juicy slab of meat: becoming president. But none of them could get close enough to grab it completely. Then you came along, with your family name *Chun,* which means "completely" in Chinese characters. While the three Kims were fighting one another for the meat at the "dog party," you grabbed it and ate it *completely,* did you not?

If any of the Kims really had true human nature, the modern history of Korea might have taken a different course. Dogs do not yield, whereas human nature is filled with the capacity to yield, understand, and help. A true politician would act through his human nature, and not with the mind of a dog, which only keeps its own interests in mind and fights over them. If a head of state rules through his human nature, he becomes an "enlightened ruler." If he rules with evil motives and selfishness, he becomes involved in a "dog party," and the nation fails.

So a politician must be guided by ethics and virtue. Only ethical politics can bring about any kind of true peace in this world. In the past, kings always recognized that, while their own expertise in politics may be developed, they still lacked understanding of true ethics and virtue. So they traditionally honored and sought out the advice of monks and learned masters, enlightened masters, people who rose to the position of "national teacher." It is very important, if a ruler is to govern effectively, that he have a clear personal philosophy.

The late President Park Chung-Hee's policies, whether judged right or wrong, had a clear direction. He emphasized filial duties and ancient Korean traditions. He reminded the Korean people of their proud past, and encouraged them to have great confidence in their work. He made them proud of something. It is true that his long reign created many undesirable side effects. But it is a fact, too, that many of his policies were directed toward reviving our pride in tradition and a strong work ethic.

President Chun, I would like to ask you what your philosophy is? It is very, very hard for me to figure it out! You should live a philosophy that emphasizes filial duties and ethics. This is the only way the Korean people can survive. Our people can survive only if every one of us recovers our self-nature.

So, President Chun, if somebody asks you, "Who are you?" how would you answer?

When Socrates was teaching Athenians to find themselves, someone asked Socrates if he knew who he was. Socrates answered, "I don't know. But I know that I don't know." This is the famous "don't-know" philosophy of Socrates.

Sir, you must find a philosophy that will guide you. If you rule the country without a philosophy and without understanding your correct direction, relying instead on selfish, partisan instincts, too many Koreans will have to suffer. President Jimmy Carter used to advocate human rights, but he failed in his endeavors mainly because he could not take any actions to back up his words. Just you or someone else saying that we need human rights and ethics is not enough. An old saying goes, "There is virtue in action, and patience in virtue." Only when there is patience can you attain a correct direction. And the universe becomes yours only when you put your true words into *action*.

But intellectual knowledge alone is not the way. Having merely intellectual knowledge is like bank employees handling money: the amount of money may be great, but it does not belong to the employees. They are handling someone else's riches! The money becomes *theirs* only when they earn it through their labor.

In the same way, people everywhere are arguing endlessly about other peoples' understanding, without making that understanding theirs. This is why our world is divided into "right" and "left." When you cut off all thinking and return to your true Self, attaining your true self-nature, there is no longer any "right" or "left," no life or death, no upper-class or lower-class.

Buddhism has very basic teachings about how we create these distinctions in our minds. When "I" exists, then "that" object exists; and when "I" doesn't exist, "that" object also does not exist. Thus this illusory "I" is the most important problem. "Who are you?" Do you understand this "I" of yours, President Chun? What is it? Tell me! Tell me!

You do not truly know now, do you? Then I ask you, how can you suppose to rule a country when you do not even know what this "I" is? How can you rule a country of millions correctly when you do not even know who you are?

Confucianism also has great teachings that can help you find your way. That is because Confucius taught that one's moral training leads to a correct management of one's household, which leads to a correct ruling of a country: world peace is possible when we are led by rulers who have attained their correct direction. Moral training comes from the training of one's mind, which is indicated by the Great Way, which is the absolute truth of the universe. Emphasizing the importance of moral training, Confucius urged his followers to abide by the Three Fundamental Principles of human relations and the Five Articles of morality. But nowadays people just ignore these teachings and fight and kill each other like animals.

So, as I have emphasized over and over again, we can expect the reunification of Korea and the attainment of world peace only when we recover our original human nature. There is no other way. As an ancient Korean history book once declared, "The world of equality, of freedom, and of peace will come only when we return to our original nature."

Thus it is of paramount importance that you attain your true "I." An ancient Chinese poem puts it this way:

> Coming empty-handed, going empty-handed—that is human.
> When you are born, where do you come from?
> When you die, where do you go?
> Life is like a floating cloud appearing in the sky;
> Death is like a floating cloud disappearing in the sky.
> The floating cloud itself originally does not exist.
> Life and death, coming and going are also like that.
> But there is one thing which always remains clear.
> It is pure and clear, not depending on life or death.

There is this "one thing" that understands that the sky is blue, while trees are green. It hears the dog when it barks, "Woof! Woof!" It tastes that salt is salty, and sugar is sweet. That "one thing" is pure and clear, and does not depend on life or death. Yes, our bodies might have life and death, but our true Self does not have life or death.

Then what is this one pure and clear thing, Mr. President? How would you answer that question? You have to be able to understand at least that point if you are going to run the country. If you cannot answer this question, then you also do not understand the correct way, truth, or correct life. Without this understanding, you could not honestly be called the leader of a country.

Jesus taught, "I am the way, truth, and correct life." The Buddha also taught the same point when he said, "When you see your true nature, you will understand the great Path, attain universal truth, and function with a correct life." So we can see that Buddhism and Christianity both have the same purpose. They just use different means to achieve that purpose, mostly because Christianity is an object-based religion whereas Buddhism seeks insight into the subject itself, the questioner: what am I?

However, some so-called Christians in Korea are always wrongly denouncing Buddhism as a religion of superstition. How foolish and narrow-minded this is! Such people do not even understand the first words of the Bible. But while teaching in the United States, I have been visited by many priests and ministers with whom I have freely discussed many aspects of our common spiritual life. We all agree that we, the religious leaders, must work hard together if we want to save all sentient beings from suffering.

President Chun, shouldn't this be the situation in Korea? Shouldn't the leaders of different religions cooperate with one another? If a house wants to prosper, there should not be any fighting among its members. Please perceive clearly the sad situation of religious relations in Korea, and promptly encourage a nationwide campaign of renewal, encouraging all to find their true nature. Such a campaign would eventually lead us closer to reunification, which would be an important step toward world peace.

President Chun, it is said that there are three dangerous tips: the tip of a sword; the tip of a tongue; and the tip of a pen. Thus it is taught that one should not surrender to the tip of a sword, one should not be conned by the tip of a tongue, and should not be deceived by the tip of a pen.

Sir, did you not stage a coup d'état with the tip of a sword? Since you did, you must of course know that it is incumbent on you to use wisely this power that you captured. If you attain that, you will have attained your Great Function, which means keeping a mind that is clear like space, and using it meticulously for others. Although our true nature is absolute, and wide, when you attain your Great Function, then sky and earth, mountain and water, upper and lower are separate and clear. When you are hungry, you must eat; when you are thirsty, you drink: these are examples of the Great Function. When a true person wins, they receive a prize; and to one who does wrong action, a penalty is given. When you come to understand this Dharma completely, you will see that actually true law contains the Great Way, justice, compassion, and ethical action. Attaining this, you will come to love and care for the whole nation as if they were no different from your own children.

Sir, do you really think you know what ethics and morals are all about? We have an unlimited supply of them already inside our own minds. If you do not know this, I suggest that you go and seek out an enlightened teacher before you think of ruling a country.

I found this out through long and hard struggle, so I wish to alert you so that you might save time and needless effort! I was born to a Presbyterian family in Pyongyang, and went to church every Sunday. When I was in high school, Koreans made up one-half of the class while Japanese made up the other half. No matter how intelligent the Korean students were, it was always a Japanese student who became the president and vice-president of the class. Actually, most of the time those who became president and vice-president of the class were among the most dim-witted students in the whole grade! But they were Japanese, and that is all that mattered at the time.

Furthermore, as you know, the Japanese tried to completely erase our history, culture, and language. They even changed our names to Japanese names and changed the national flag. My hatred toward the Japanese was so intense that I fought with Japanese students every day, and I was punished by the Japanese teachers every day.

Then, one day I met a member of the Korea Free Army. I immediately stole money from my family and traveled northward to Harbin to join the resistance, along with a friend. Arriving in Harbin, I went to see my friend's brother, who had graduated from a Japanese university and owned a rice mill there. When I bragged about my joining the resistance army, he flew into a rage and shouted, "You little runt, you! What do you understand about resistance and independence, huh? Independence work is not accomplished by emotion alone! It is possible only when your wisdom, emotion, and consciousness become one. You must also have a correct insight into life and the nature of the universe. With self-knowledge such as this, the correct action will always appear. Understand?" He also told me that, since the "three tips" were greatly to be feared, I must return to Pyongyang and study until my "center" became strong, and my mind was not moving.

So from this experience, I must say to you: we must find our true nature so that we do not surrender to the tip of a sword, nor be fooled by the tip of a tongue, nor be deceived by the tip of a pen. For was it not the power of these "three tips" that created the existence of "communism" and "capitalism" in the first place, and then drew humanity into this war that threatens to destroy the world? So it must be clear that we must overcome the grave danger of these "three tips," and to do that we must return to our original nature.

But since you do not even know what your "I" is, Mr. President, I encourage you to seek out and question an enlightened person about the nature of ethical politics.

Yet you should not be fooled by mere intellectual knowledge of this matter: conceptual knowledge is still not true wisdom. When I was on the board of directors of Dongguk University, the largest Buddhist university in the country, I tried to locate for the university a person who had both scholarship and real virtue. I found many, many people who excelled in their scholastic fields, but could find no one in academia who combined great scholarship with true virtue and morals. My point is, we cannot expect scholars to guide the country well, since mere knowledge and learning do not have any real power. Most scholars are only filled with dry, empty cognition. You must understand that in school settings, we only accumulate more and more knowledge, whereas true wisdom comes from direct insight into our self-nature. Wisdom of this kind leads directly to moral behavior, and virtue.

Book knowledge is like having a tape recorder: everything recorded belongs to someone else. That is only someone else's ideas, which you have collected. But we can see clearly and live clearly only when we have wisdom, which leads to a compassion that saves all beings from suffering.

Sir, in our long history there have been many Zen masters who combined their insight with correct intellectual knowledge to make wisdom and morals. Such people always appeared whenever the nation was in need of them, at moments of great peril. The great Master Won Hyo Sunim of the Shilla Dynasty was such a one, as was National Teacher Bo Myong from the Koryo Dynasty, Masters Seo Sahn and Sah Myong of the Yi Dynasty, and Zen Masters Kyong Ho and Man Gong in our early modern period. During the colonial occupation and right after liberation from Japan, we have seen Zen Masters Dong Sahn, Hyo Bong, Keum Oh, Hyong Dahm, Kyong Sahn, and Kyong Bong, all great lights who have passed on in recent years.

Although we have lost many great masters recently, there are yet several more still practicing and teaching in Korea. Many people travel deep into the mountains to learn wisdom and morals from these teachers. They are the treasures of the nation, Mr. President, who would be praised as saints if they had lived in the West. Unfortunately, because politics in Korea are so cutthroat, these three masters have made a firm decision not to get involved in worldly affairs, and have left the secular world you inhabit. Sir, for the sake of the Korean people, please visit these three masters to ask and learn about correct wisdom and the nature of moral action. Please lead your countrymen in a correct direction by first attaining your true nature.

You probably know of these three masters: one of them is the great Zen Master Soeng Chol, who has thrown away the world completely and stays at Baek Ryon Am hermitage deep inside Kaya Sahn Mountain, behind Hae In Sah Temple. He has vowed never to leave the mountain.

The second master has a very good understanding of Confucianism, Buddhism, and Taoism. His name is Master Tan Ho, and he lives at Weol Jeong Sah Temple in O Dae Sahn Mountain.

The third master is Kwan Ung Sunim, who resides at Yu Ji Sah Temple in Hwang Ak Sahn Mountain.

I dearly wish that you attain your correct wisdom, Mr. President, and that means seeking out these great masters. Ask them for their teachings, and they will teach you how to find your original nature. Who can guarantee that even you will live until tomorrow or the day after? A man who dies has no use for country, or citizens, or family, or even the reunification of North and South Korea or world peace. Yet wasn't it Confucius who said, "If I attain the Way in the morning, I will not regret dying the evening of the same day"? And the Buddha taught us that when one attains one's self-nature, there is no longer any life or death, and thus there is nothing to be afraid of. Rather, there is only the wish to save all beings from suffering, not only in this life, but in life after life. We call this the Great Bodhisattva Way: giving all of oneself for the benefit of sentient beings. The three masters above can show you how to attain this!

Sir, I do not know if there are truly enlightened people in other religions alive today. If there are, please feel free to seek them out, if you wish, and strive together with them to help our country in these difficult times. When you are able to do this, then all our people will be united and have the correct direction with which we can achieve the reunification of Korea. This will plant the seed of world peace.

History tells us that when a country's religions functioned correctly, that country prospered. When those religions were corrupted, so was the country, in some important ways. This has been the case in all countries in every period of history. Just look at what is happening in the Muslim countries, and even in the United States and Japan. Because religions in those places have fallen into a state of confusion in which their original message has been perverted for impure ends, consequently the politics, culture, and to some extent the economies have lost their direction.

This is why it is extremely important to abandon the thinking that "my religion is superior to yours." This is why it is of paramount importance that we find our correct human nature. We can have correct religious life, correct politics, a correct economic system, and correct cultural values *only* when people are making an effort to attain their true nature. When you let go of your opinion, condition, and situation, self-nature will appear spontaneously, shining like the sun. Then this very world will be transformed into a paradise, right where you stand.

Don't you recognize that you live in a world that is constantly changing, changing, changing, changing, nonstop? This whole existence is fraught with change; it cannot be believed. So therefore you must attain your true root; you must attain the nature of the ground on which you now stand. Even a child knows that a tree without roots cannot stand! It will soon fall down.

You are president, yet you must also sense the mood of the people, and determine what they really want. This is your root, as president. You have to see with your *eyes* the changing conditions in which your people live and work. You must use your *ears* to know the movement of their minds, and hear their complaints. You must use your *nose* to sense the direction of their mood, to perceive the winds of change blowing through our society and our world. You must use your *tongue* to know the taste of what you yourself are doing, from moment to moment. And you must use your *body* to act for them.

You can only last long as president if your body can find its root, and then know the ground on which you stand. I ask you to please find this root. You must ask yourself, "What is my root?" "When was my root made?" "Who made my root?" You must ask yourself this, very deeply. Only then will you be able to perceive your direction and this whole society's correct direction. From this kind of study alone can Korea survive, and if through your example other leaders come to study like this, we will truly attain world peace. The point is that world peace appears when people in power lead the correct way.

Mr. President, it is said that blood is thicker than water. Though I have lived mostly outside Korea for the last twenty years, teaching in Japan and the West, the well-being of Korea and her people have always been paramount in my mind. Actually, it does not matter to me who or what party is in power, if you want to know the truth. My wish has always been and will always be that my homeland, Korea, be prosperous and strong.

Sir, please go to visit one of these great enlightened masters and attain wisdom. Please recover your human nature and become the guiding light of the Korean people. If Koreans have such a light to follow, can we doubt that the dawn of reunification is far away?

Wishing your continued health, and the realization of all your wishes,

> *The Han River's waters have been flowing for hundreds of*
> *years;*
> *Sam Gak Sahn Mountain* has watched us since time*
> *immemorial.*

In the Dharma,
Seung Sahn Haeng Won

---

*Sam Gak Sahn Mountain, a prominent peak on the outskirts of Seoul, is the mountain where Hwa Gye Sah Temple is located.

THE EARLY LIFE OF
ZEN MASTER SEUNG SAHN

Zen Master Seung Sahn was born Lee Duk-In on July 4, 1927, in the village of Sun-Cheon, north of Pyongyang, in what is now North Korea. His father was a civil engineer, and his parents were both devout Presbyterians.

In his teen years, Duk-In studied at the Pyongyang Industrial School. He had a knack for fixing things, and he quickly earned the nickname "Edison's Dreamer," owing to his ability to repair broken clocks and radios and fashion workable machines out of discarded materials.

Duk-In grew up in the hostile environment of a Japanese-occupied Korea—an occupation that lasted from 1910 to 1945. During this occupation, Koreans were forbidden to speak their own language and were required to adopt Japanese names. Many students were forced to work in the Japanese factories, supporting Japan's war efforts.

One of Duk-In's schoolteachers taught him how to build shortwave radios and other telegraphic machines—technical knowledge that was denied to nearly all Koreans at the time. Duk-In ended up using his technical skills to gather information on Japanese armaments factories and troop movements, and he passed this information along to leaders in the Korean resistance movement. He was eventually arrested for aiding the resistance and sent to prison in Pyongyang.

In Japanese-occupied Korea, the torture and killing of political prisoners was commonplace. While in prison, Duk-In was interrogated each week, and though his captors did not torture him, they used threats, manipulation, and intimidation to try to break him down.

While in prison, Duk-In began to have grave questions about the Christian religion in which he had been raised. "If there was a loving God," he recalled thinking, "how could he permit the Koreans to suffer so much?"

Suddenly, in the late spring of 1944, after four and a half months of imprisonment, Duk-In was freed, due in large part to the intercession of one of his teachers, and the head of his school, both of whom believed in the young man's great future promise. He later learned that he had gained release from a death sentence, which would have been carried out on the day he turned eighteen.

After his release from prison, Duk-In graduated from school and was admitted to Dae Dong Industrial College. The war ended several months later. Soon groups of Communists, with the collusion of their Soviet supporters, began to rally and organize local cells. They hounded landowners and students, and so, owing to his family's background, Duk-In was constantly harassed. With his name frequently appearing on lists of suspected opponents, his friends and family urged him to flee. Reluctantly, and with time running out, he joined a historic flood of tens of thousands of others fleeing Communist rule. He headed down to what is now South Korea, vowing to return when the situation improved.

It never has. He never saw his family again. In 1946 he entered Dong Guk University, which was the only Buddhist university in Seoul and one of the leading universities in Korea. He supported himself by putting his engineering skills to work fixing gadgets and electronics.

Duk-In saved money and formed a group to support other refugees from the north, who were beginning to suffer discrimination at the hands of their southern brethren. Meanwhile the political situation was increasingly unstable. As daily life became more violent and chaotic, and the newly free society collapsed around him, Duk-In lost all faith in human beings and went to the mountains, vowing never to return until he had attained the truth that would save his people.

In Korea there is an old tradition of temples providing room and board for students and civil servants who are studying for exams, and it was in such hermitages that Duk-In sought refuge for a brief period. At this time Duk-In had no intention of becoming a Buddhist monk—he only wished to find answers through deep engagement with the classics of Western philosophy and Confucianism. He thought Buddhism was involved more with superstitious practices than any authentic search for truth. But in his studies he eventually became dissatisfied with the politics of Confucian thought and the metaphysics of Western thought. After three months of intensive Confucian study, he returned to the Buddhist hermitage Sang Won Am to study Buddhism.

When he asked the abbot for teachings in Buddhism, he was given a musty, yellowed copy of the *Diamond Sutra*. Opening it up, he read the words, "All things that appear in this world are illusion. If you view all appearance as nonappearance, then you will see your true nature." He said that he immediately felt a great burden lifted, a long discontent dropping away. He soon came to believe that all Buddhist teaching could be found in this one phrase.

One day, while sitting in the woods reading the *Diamond Sutra*, he encountered an older monk who asked why he was studying Buddhism. Duk-In said, "I believe that our society has become completely rotten, Sunim. Human beings have lost their way, but I believe that through learning Buddhism I can learn how to help humanity."

"You cannot save anyone by learning Buddhism. That is because Buddhism is not concerned with understanding."

These words shocked Duk-In. For a moment he was not sure that he had heard correctly. So he asked, "Then what is the way to study Buddhism?"

The monk continued, "True study of Buddhism is not concerned with learning more things. Buddhist study is about cutting off completely the mistaken notion of self. You must let go of all thinking. Only in this way can you attain your true self. Only forget your false notion of self."

Duk-In was inspired by this exchange to become a monk. But he faced one grave problem: he was the only son in his family. If he became a monk, his family line would come to an end. He resolved that, though it would shame his family if he became a monk, if he practiced hard and attained his true self, this would serve his family greater than anything he could achieve as a mere householder.

Duk-In was ordained as a Buddhist monk in October 1948. He immediately went into the mountains on a hundred-day chanting retreat. He ate only pine needles, ground into a powder. For twenty hours every day he chanted the Great Dharani (a very long mantra). He took only ice-cold baths.

At first he was filled with doubt and almost gave up several times. Then he was visited by a variety of demons and ghosts, and then by Buddhas and Bodhisattvas. At a certain point two spirits in the shape of young boys appeared and accompanied him on either side when he went for walks. Throughout it all he kept a strong practice, only chanting. His skin turned green from the pine needles, and gradually his body became stronger.

Finally it was the last day. He was outside chanting and hitting the *moktak* (wooden drum) when suddenly his body disappeared. From far away he could hear the beat of the *moktak* and the sound of his own voice. After some time in this state, he returned to his body, and he understood: the rocks, the river, everything he could see and hear, all were his true self. The truth is just like this.

When he came down from the mountain, he met with the great Zen master Ko Bong. But Ko Bong declined to be his teacher because he was mainly teaching laypeople at that time, having determined that many monks were either lazy or arrogant.

But when he returned to Zen Master Ko Bong, there was still one *kong-an* (or *koan,* a Zen teaching question) that he could not answer right away: "The mouse eats cat food, but the cat bowl is broken. What does this mean?" He tried and tried, and gave many answers, but Ko Bong Sunim rejected them all. Then, all of a sudden, the correct answer appeared. The young monk had attained enlightenment! Soon after that, Ko Bong Sunim gave his young student the transmission of dharma. He was given the name Seung Sahn (Exalted Mountain), and his teacher foresaw Seung Sahn Sunim spreading his teaching throughout the world. Seung Sahn was the only person to whom Zen Master Ko Bong ever gave transmission.

At the age of twenty-two, he was now a Zen master.

ABOUT THE EDITOR

Hyon Gak Sunim, a Zen monk, was born Paul Muenzen in Rahway, New Jersey. Educated at Yale College and Harvard University, he was ordained a monk under Zen Master Seung Sahn in 1992 at Nam Hwa Sah Temple, the temple of the Sixth Patriarch, Guangzhou, People's Republic of China. He has compiled and edited a number of Zen Master Seung Sahn's texts, including *The Compass of Zen* and *Only Don't Know*. He received *inka* from Zen Master Seung Sahn in 2001, and is currently guiding teacher of the Seoul International Zen Center at Hwa Gye Sah Temple, Seoul.

To find a Zen center or group near you, contact

THE KWAN UM SCHOOL OF ZEN
99 Pound Road
Cumberland, RI 02864-2726
Tel.: (401) 658-1464
Fax: (401) 658-1188
E-mail: info@kwanumzen.org
Website: www.kwanumzen.com